# A Modern Approach to Quilt Design
# improv
# paper piecing

## Amy Friend

Published in 2017 by Lucky Spool Media, LLC

www.luckyspool.com
info@luckyspool.com

Text © Amy Friend
Editor: Susanne Woods
Designer: Page + Pixel
Illustrator: Kari Vojtechovsky
Photographer: © Amy Friend

9 8 7 6 5 4 3 2 1
First Edition
Printed in China

Library of Congress Cataloging-in-
Publication Data available upon request

ISBN 978-1-940655-23-9
LSID0035

This book is dedicated to all makers who are ready to take a creative risk.

# table of
# contents

# Introduction

A statement like "there are no truly original ideas" is so discouraging and defeating to the creative spirit. Maybe it is true, and maybe it is not, but we are all individuals who approach design and execution of that design with our own unique talents, skills, aesthetics, and vision. Because of that, it is indeed possible for you to create a final product that is truly yours. The sense of satisfaction and fulfillment that comes from allowing yourself to pursue creativity and take chances is immense. I may not be a risk taker in my day-to-day life, but I am in my art. Why not, right? There is so much possibility and nothing to lose.

In this book, I use paper piecing, a standard quilting technique, for all of the projects. If this is a new technique for you, see my *Paper-Piecing Essentials* on page 12. Some of my designs are based on traditional blocks that have been around forever, but I approach paper-pieced quilt design with a new twist to create one-of-a-kind modern quilts. I hope that this book will encourage you to explore my techniques and combine them with your personal vision to create some amazing quilted art.

# What is Improvisational Paper Piecing?

When I think of paper piecing, I think of precision—yet the word improvisation brings to mind a process full of creative freedom and unexpected results. "Improvisational paper piecing" sounds like an oxymoron, doesn't it? Let me explain.

What initially drew me to paper piecing was not only the precision that was possible, but even moreso the design possibilities. I was not limited to shapes that could be easily defined by standard measurements and specific angles before being rotary cut, and creative opportunities really opened up for me. It became possible to sew asymmetrical shapes, pieces cut on the bias, and hard-to-measure acute triangles. Over the last few years, the design process I've used to create some of my favorite quilts has been improvisationally "flavored." I use paper piecing because it works on a template principle where each pattern can be reproduced. Combined with the freedom of improv, this technique allows me to produce unique and creative designs that can then be *repeated*.

## Improvisation

Improvisation is usually defined as work created without preparation or planning. In the case of quilting, it often refers to a process that isn't guided by a pattern, where fabric is not measured, but cut freehand. Improvisation doesn't mean there aren't any rules. Most successful improvisational works have some guidelines established by the maker. In this case, because we are working with paper-pieced blocks, our guidelines are determined by the *technique*. In order to paper piece, we need to have straight stitching lines and a sewable order.

## Paper Piecing

Paper piecing, or foundation piecing, is a method of sewing quilt blocks where the design is printed on a paper foundation. On that foundation, the sections are numbered in the appropriate sewing order. Fabric is positioned on the back of the foundation, with right sides together. The seam is stitched on the sewing line located on the front of the foundation. The seam allowance is trimmed and the fabric opened out and pressed. This process continues in numerical order until all sections are covered in fabric. Sometimes,

it is necessary to break a block into a few larger sections that are each pieced and then stitched together. The resulting block is a mirror image of the foundation pattern. So, typically, a mirror image of the pattern is made prior to sewing so that the end result matches your original vision. For more information see "Paper Piecing Essentials" (page 12) and "How to Group and Number Paper-Pieced Templates" (page 14).

This book shares three approaches to improvisational paper-pieced design and includes nine modern quilt patterns to illustrate these methods. All of the templates for the patterns and directions for how to make them are included. You can recreate the quilts, but my main goal is to inspire you to learn from each quilt's design process and to use the prompts in the back of this book to create your own improvisational paper-pieced designs.

In all three approaches, the goal is to embrace the free, askew, asymmetrical, irregular style of improvisational sketching. When drawing, you may want to exaggerate the slant of your lines and purposely go off-center, intentionally mimicking the improv piecing style.

## The Goals of the Book

You might ask: Why the need to paper piece? Repetition often draws us into quilts due to the primary and secondary patterns a repeated unit creates. A quick flip through a book of traditional quilts will illustrate this. The blocks meet at seam lines, creating new shapes (i.e., secondary patterns) through the joining of blocks.

The ability to play with pattern, to control the placement and contrast of fabrics from light to dark, to combine decades-old block designs with just the right fabrics and just the right arrangement so that they look surprisingly different and modern—this, the ability to repeat an improvisationally drawn block with the precision of paper piecing, is what makes this technique exciting.

For example, the traditional Maltese Cross block (Fig. 1) is interesting on its own. But when it is connected to other identical units, it forms a secondary pattern of squares within squares on point where the blocks meet at the corners (Fig. 2). And a circular pattern emerges, formed by the diamond shapes from connecting blocks. Normally, one pattern will dominate and catch the eye first, drawing it across the quilt.

Figure 1

Figure 2

Repetition of improvisationally designed paper-pieced blocks works similarly. The eye focuses on key design elements and travels across the quilt, noting the repetition of shape.

This Kite Tails block (Fig. 3) is an example of my improvisationally designed paper piecing. The accompanying layout shows it repeated, with some blocks inverted (Fig. 4). When I look at this top, my eye homes in on one particularly wonky shape in the negative space

created between two kite tails (Fig. 5). This bit of negative space is dominant. It creates tension and interest.

By creating a block from an improvisational sketch and then repeating it methodically with paper piecing, you harness the power of repetitive design. But, because the block design is improvisational, the patterns feel fresh and unexpected.

Figure 3

Figure 4

Figure 5

# Paper-Piecing Essentials

Prior to moving into paper-pieced block design, it is important to understand the basics. So, let's practice using a familiar Flying Geese block (see page 122).

Begin with your template. You can choose to print it on specialty foundation piecing paper or copy paper (I use copy paper myself.). Make sure that you are beginning with a foundation of the proper size. It's so discouraging to spend time piecing a block only to discover that it isn't the right size and can't be used for your project. Take care to enlarge to the correct percentage too.

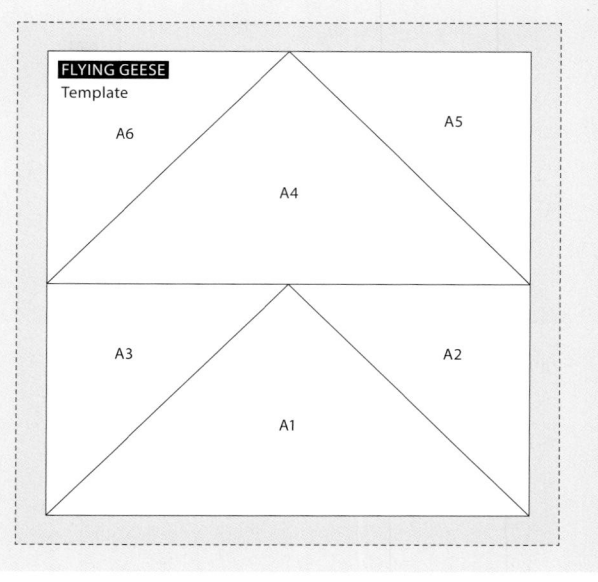

**FLYING GEESE** Template

1. When paper piecing, we work on the reverse side of the paper. This means that our finished block will be a mirror image of the foundation pattern. To begin, cover section A1 with fabric pinned to the wrong side of the foundation paper. Position the fabric to extend at least ¼" beyond all the stitching lines by holding it up to a light source (Fig. 1). The right side of the fabric should be facing up, and the wrong side against the paper.

2. Place the fabric for Section A2 on top of the fabric for Section A1, right sides together, extending at least ¼" beyond the seam line. Pin in place if needed (Fig. 2). Fold the fabric back along the seam line to make sure it covers Section A2 prior to stitching your seam. Flip over your template so that the numbers are facing you and the fabric is on the bottom.

3. Prior to sewing, change to a size 90 sewing-machine needle and set your stitch length to 1.6–1.8 mm. This will make bigger punctures and more perforations in your foundation paper and will make paper removal easier. Stitch along the seam line between A1 and A2, extending into the seam allowance at both ends.

Fold the paper along the sewn line so that the right side of the paper is facing. Use a ruler to measure ¼" away from the sewn line onto the exposed fabric. Trim off the excess fabric with a rotary cutter and press open.

4–6. Repeat this process for all of the template sections, being sure to work in numerical order (Figs. 3-7).

7. With the paper side facing up, trim around the template. Make sure to include any marked seam allowance.

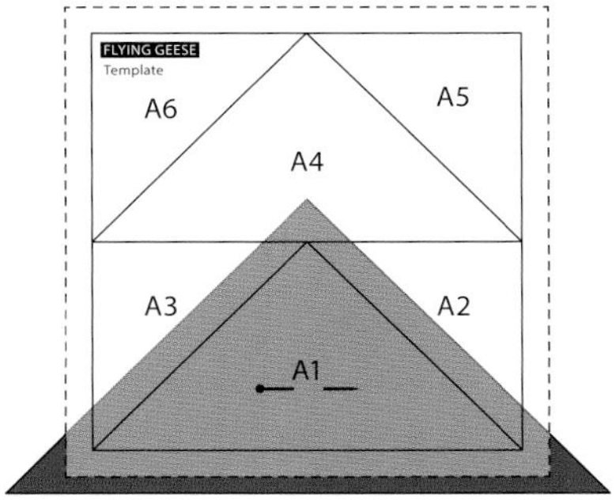

**Figure 1**

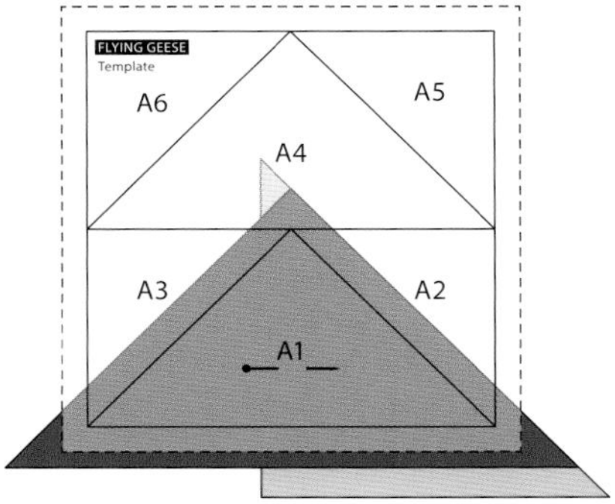

**Figure 2**

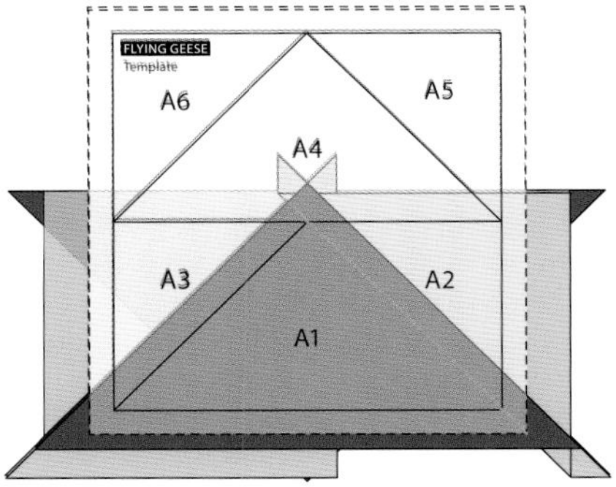

**Figure 3**

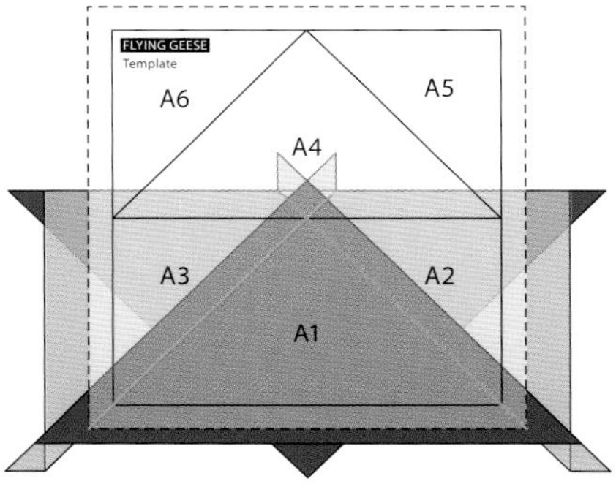

**Figure 4**

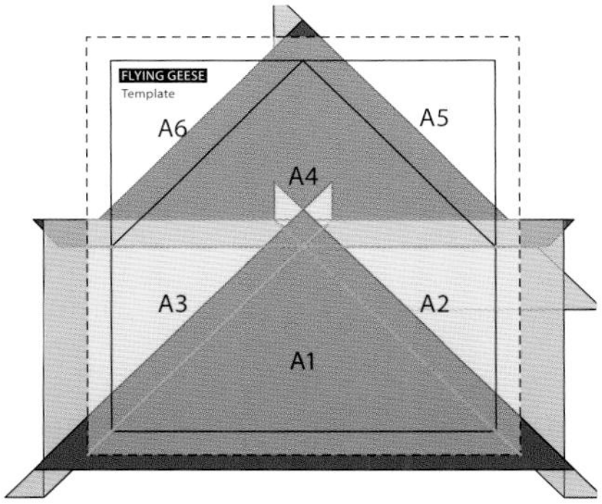

**Figure 5**

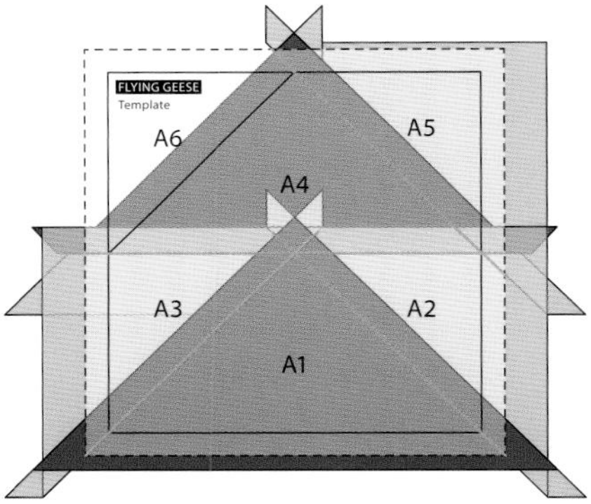

**Figure 6**

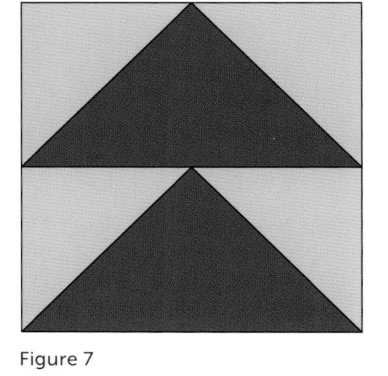

**Figure 7**

*By immersing yourself in the paper-piecing process, you will come to understand how pattern sections are grouped and numbered without even realizing it.*

# How to Group and Number Paper-Pieced Templates

Because you will be designing your own paper-pieced blocks, it is important to understand how to group and number sections. If you are familiar with paper piecing, this will come easily to you. Truly, the best preparation for designing your own blocks is to sew blocks designed, grouped and numbered by others. By immersing yourself in the paper-piecing process, you will come to understand how pattern sections are grouped and numbered without even realizing it. The process becomes intuitive.

To practice, we will group and number two traditional blocks. Both blocks can be traditionally pieced and I chose them for that reason. A background in traditional piecing will help make the reasoning behind the numbering order more clear. If you fall in love with this method, adapt any traditional block to paper piecing to add precision!

The basic concept is this: groups are assigned a letter, and then within the group the piecing order is established through numbering.

## Southern Belle

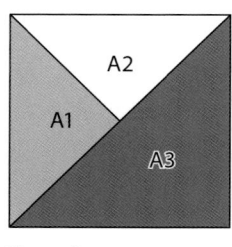

Figure 1

Figure 2

Begin by looking at the Southern Belle block. If you have experience piecing blocks, you will probably see that each quadrant of the block is identical. So let's isolate just one quadrant.

Look at these three pieces and consider which seam needs to be sewn first (Fig. 1). I picture the process of flipping the fabric from one section to another. The seam between the two smaller triangles needs to be pieced first

(Fig. 2). It doesn't matter which is numbered A1 and which is A2. After these two sections are pieced, the final section is A3.

The numbering system establishes the sewing order, not colors. It can help though, to create a block diagram with corresponding sections colored to suggest your intended fabric selections. Then consult the diagram when selecting fabric in order to place it properly.

## Triangle Weave

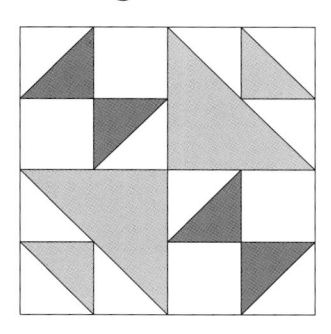

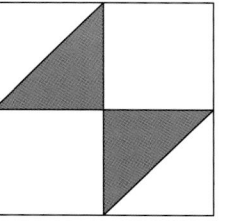

Figure 3

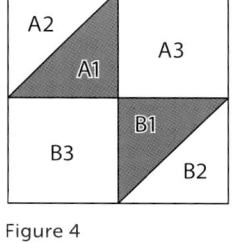

Figure 4

Figure 5

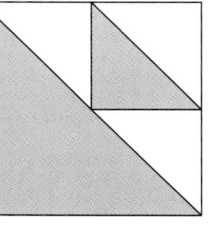

Figure 6

Next, let's look at the more complex Triangle Weave block. There are two distinctly different quadrants, both of which are repeated to create the block.

Let's start with the upper left quadrant (Fig. 3). This quadrant cannot be sewn as one section. We will need to number the half-square triangles A1 and A2, then the adjacent square A3. The bottom of the block will be another group similarly numbered B1, B2, and B3. The maker will piece and trim these two groups and then sew them together to create the upper left quadrant of the block (Fig. 4).

I could have grouped Sections A and B vertically, which would also work. These are choices that, you, the designer makes.

Moving to the second quadrant, I can see that it will be possible to piece it in one large section that I will label Group C (Fig. 5).

The outer half-square-triangle unit needs to be pieced first, so those will be numbered C1 and C2. (Again, which is which, is a matter of preference.) Then the two outer triangles can be sewn. They are numbered C3 and C4 (again, interchangeably). The final larger triangle is C5 (Fig. 6).

With these basics reviewed, we are ready to move on, get into the improv mindset and design our own blocks!

# Getting into the Improv Mindset

In addition to channeling an improvisational style in block designs, approach your design work with an improv mindset. Whether you're working on paper or using design software to sketch blocks, your mind should be free of too many preconceived notions or expectations and your drawing arm relaxed.

Get out a scribble pad and sketch mindlessly for a bit; doodle! These sketches are not to be saved or shown to others. Their sole purpose is to relax your arm so don't worry about what they look like! If this sort of exercise doesn't come naturally to you, it might help to find a large sheet of paper and challenge yourself to go big with your doodles and really move your arm.

Begin by making a series of loop-de-loops across the page. Make a row or two, and then move on to another simple shape such as a circle or oval. While drawing the shape, continue around and around until it appears well formed, allowing your lines to crisscross and overlap. Or draw a series of closely spaced imperfect circles, much like free-motion quilted pebbles. Try sketching some spirals. While you do all this, do not strive for perfection. Just focus on letting your arm move freely.

Since paper piecing requires straight lines, switching gears at this point can help prepare you for the next step. Try some straight-line doodles. Do you doodle while on hold during a phone call? When I do, I tend to draw interlocking squares or stacking triangles. Try a series of those. Then make some simple crosshatch grids. Again, you should not be attempting to make your lines ruler straight or precise in any way. Just focus on making marks on your page that will promptly go into the trash after they have served their purpose: freeing your arm and mind to sketch improvisationally.

Once your drawing arm is loosened up, sketch a block design and embrace the results. Only change the lines if it is necessary to do so in order to actually construct the block. Acknowledge the paper-piecing constraint and use that limitation to your advantage. It is okay to use a ruler to straighten sketched lines—but if the lines are not parallel, or are unevenly spaced or askew, leave that spacing as you originally drew it. That's what we want! Resist the temptation to listen to your inner perfectionist in the design phase; save that for the paper-piecing part!

## sketchbook

Find a sketchbook with fairly large sheets, especially if you tend to be tight. Force your arm to loosen up and move freely across the entire page. Don't feel the need to spend a lot on high quality paper, because this is just a warming up exercise. That said, sometimes great things come from doodles, so you might want a bound sketchbook format for that reason.

## PEN OR PENcil

I prefer a pen because using a pen prevents you from erasing imperfections. I love the Pigma Brush Pen because it makes bold marks and responds nicely with variances of line weight from the pressure you apply to the pen. If using a pencil, choose a soft lead such as an HB and promise to keep that eraser out of sight!

# How to Design Your Own Improv Block Templates

I am going to describe the process of designing an improv block template using my *Kite Tails* block design as an example (see pages 140-141). The ideas behind my design process will be covered in detail in the subsequent chapters, but I will say that my inspiration here was the bits of fabric or ribbon tied to a kite string. I established a couple of guidelines for my design. I wanted my block size to be big and rectangular. And I wanted the kite tails to vary in size and shape but to meet along the center seam, though not at a point.

1. Draw a rectangle 12″ × 18″ (Fig. 1).

2. Divide the rectangle vertically along the center line (Fig. 2).

3. Improvisationally sketch bow-tie-like shapes that meet at the center seam (Fig. 3). Do not make all your lines follow the same angle or be spaced the same distance apart. If you start to run out of space, you will be forced to make a final skinny bow shape. Go with it!

4. Once your block is designed, it is time to group, number and color (optional). For this design, it is clear that we will need to create two groups, A and B, for the left and right halves of the block. Within those two groups, we can number the pieces in consecutive order (Fig. 4).

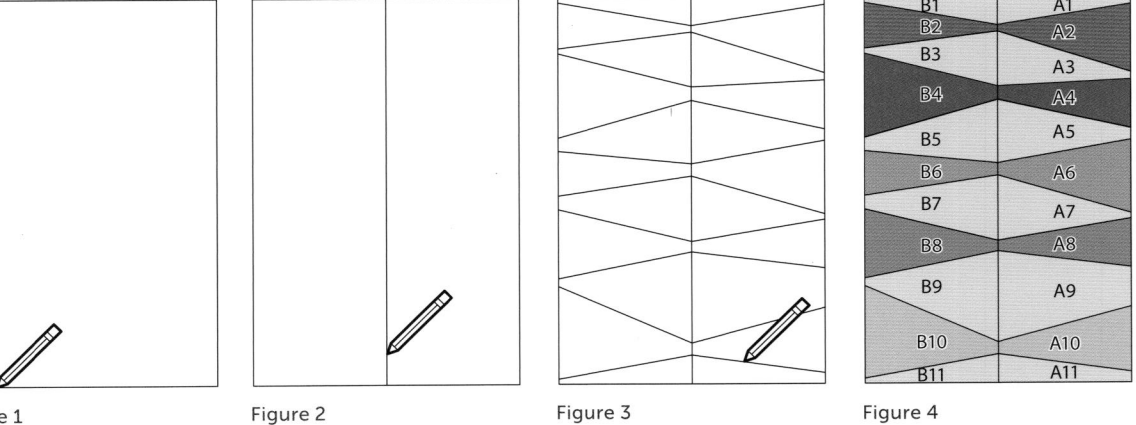

Figure 1          Figure 2          Figure 3          Figure 4

### Construction Order

When the ordering of pieces is irrelevant and your hand is not forced by the constraints of construction order, there are a few piecing factors you can consider. If you want to use a directional print or a stripe or otherwise, fussy cut a certain piece in your block design, consider numbering that piece "1," if possible. You will be able to fussy cut most easily by simply holding the foundation paper to the light and placing your fabric precisely within the space of that segment.

You might also consider the value of your fabrics. If you have the option of piecing the lighter fabric first and then the darker, the seam allowances will be hidden when you press your pieces to the dark side of the fabric. Perhaps the direction in which your pieces are sewn might make it possible to nest groups together? Or maybe a particular piece is an awkward size. It's nice, if you have the choice, to start with that piece. These are all more advanced numbering choices that are not always necessary to consider, but can be worthwhile.

## Preparing the Pattern

Once your pieces are grouped and numbered, it's time to prepare the pattern for duplication and piecing. The pattern must be the mirror image of your original, groups must be separated into sections, and seam allowances need to be added to all of the sides of each section. If you are using quilt design software, it is easy to do this in just a few steps, but it is also possible to simply use paper, a pencil and a ruler.

The mirror image can be created in a couple of ways. Using photo editing software or apps, you can select image rotation and "flip canvas horizontal". You could also place your paper face down against a light source such as a light table or a window, and trace the lines on the back of the page, making that your mirror image template. If you choose that latter method, be sure to use a ruler when tracing so your lines remain straight and accurate.

The next step is to separate the pattern into Sections A, B, C, etc. If you are using photo editing software, you can separate your sections by cropping and saving each group individually. If you are working with paper and pencil, trace each Section separately or photocopy your design and cut around each Section to isolate them. Using the ¼˝ line on a clear acrylic ruler, add a seam allowance all the way around each group (Fig. 5).

Now you are ready to duplicate your pattern pieces; simply said, it's time to make copies! If you are printing from quilt-design software, make sure you are printing your PDF at 100% or set scaling to "none." When making photocopies from hand-drawn patterns, also make sure that they are printing at 100% or actual size.

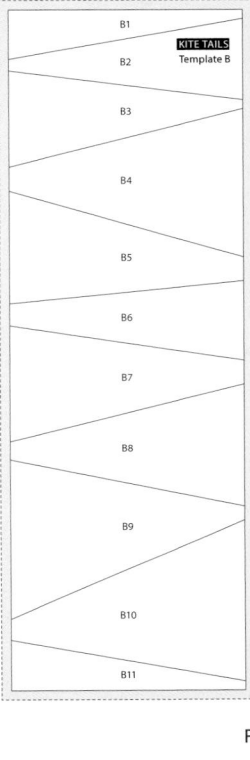
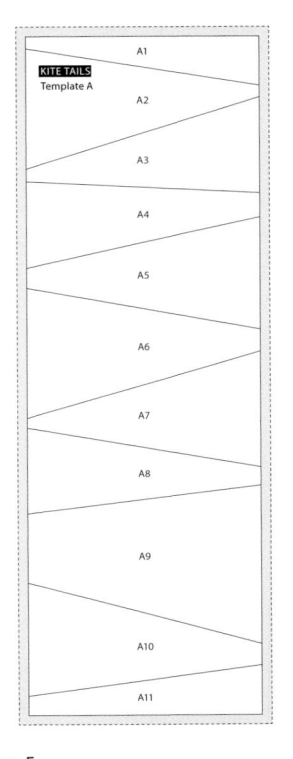

Figure 5

# Advanced Paper-Piecing Tips

Prior to moving on, I want to share a few paper-piecing tips with you. Fabric is cut generously for paper piecing in order to make fabric placement easier. The fabric waste created is worth it because it makes the piecing so much simpler and more enjoyable.

Typically, I measure sections across the widest point and the longest point of each piece and cut my fabric to those dimensions plus about an inch. If I am paper piecing a half-square triangle, I will measure one side of it, add about an inch, cut a square that size, and then bisect it to avoid fabric waste.

But with improv paper-pieced blocks, the sections are often very irregularly shaped. It is still possible to piece them using the guidelines for fabric cutting mentioned above, but there will be quite a bit of waste. I have found that it is often helpful to work from a width of fabric and then take advantage of the angles cut while piecing in order to piece the next section. This is particularly effective when working with solids that do not have obvious

right and wrong sides, but you can sometimes use the technique with prints too. Let me illustrate this idea using the *Kite Tails* block once again. Of course, the exact way in which you do this will depend on your block design.

In this instance, I have found that it is most efficient to work on Sections A and B simultaneously, using pieces of fabric that are cut to about 8˝ × 16˝.

I begin by pinning the background fabric to Sections A1 and B1 (Fig. 1). Then, I use the head of a pin to mark both ends of the seam line between these sections and A2 and B2.

Next, working on the fabric side of my foundation, I the fold the print that will cover Section A2 under, so that it will match the seam line that I marked with pins. This allows me to see exactly how the section will look once sewn so I can adjust any directional prints (Fig. 2). Then I reach my hand under the printed fabric and flip it over so right sides are facing.

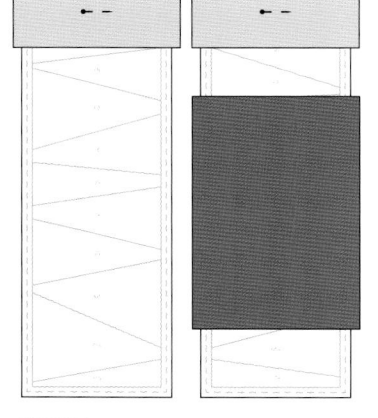

Figure 1

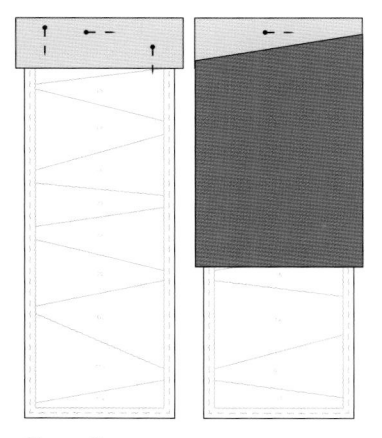

Figure 2

Next, I flip the block and stitch along the seam line between Sections A1 and A2. Then I mark the seam line between A2 and A3 at both ends and repeat this process with the background fabric (Fig. 3), leaving the length of the printed fabric there until I trim the seam between A2 and A3 (Fig. 4).

See how the angle of the trimmed fabric works fairly well with Section B2 (Fig. 5)?

Repeat this process to piece Section B2. The background fabric will be placed in the same manner, also taking advantage of the angle cut for efficiency and fabric placement.

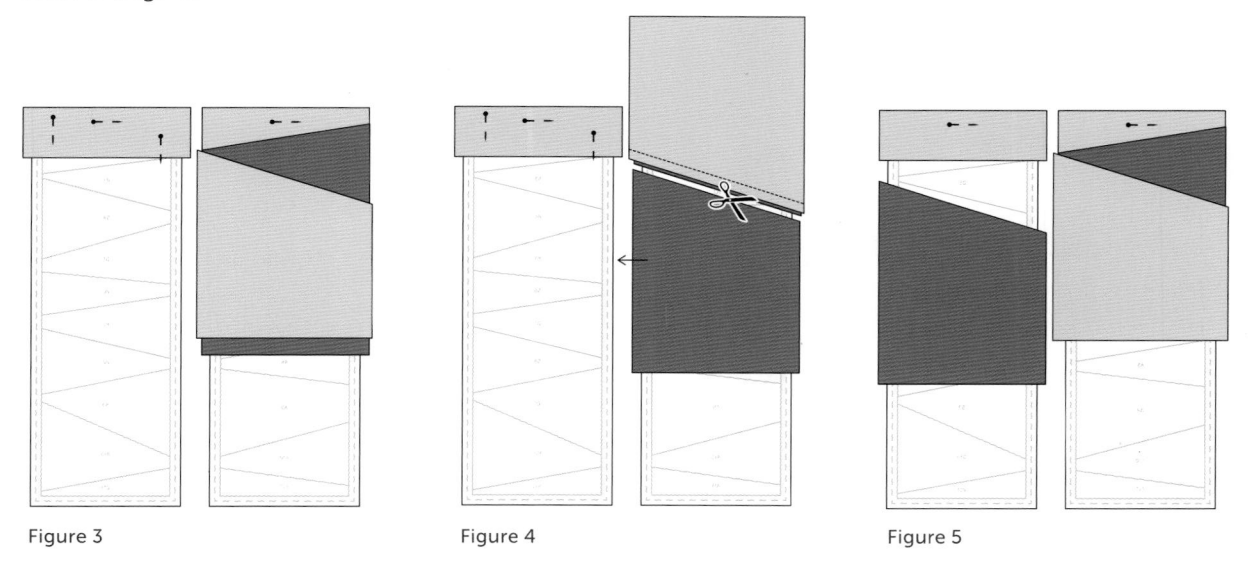

Figure 3

Figure 4

Figure 5

# Be Inspired by Tradition

This is a fantastic starting point for improv drafting of paper pieced blocks. The wonky look is familiar to many of us as one of the starting points of modern quilt desgin in general (we all remember those wonky stars from 2010, like in Figure 1, right?). Quilters often make stars with improvisationally pieced points using an unmeasured stitch-and-flip technique to create the arms of the star.

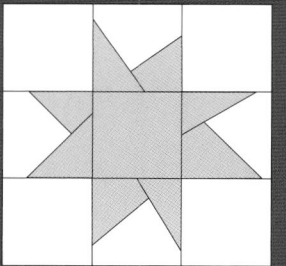

Figure 1

You've seen improvisationally pieced Flying Geese (Fig. 2) and wonky Log Cabins (Fig. 4)? The signature style of these pieces is asymmetry, skewed lines and lack of parallel lines.

To experiment with drafting your own patterns, first look for a traditional block that is simple in construction (Figs. 3 and 5). Sketch it quickly with an improvisational style, with lines that are not parallel and blocks that are not symmetrical. Often, unexpectedly wonky shapes will result. Resist the temptation to "fix" perceived flaws in the sketch; instead, see where they might lead.

Figure 2      Figure 3

Complex blocks are not as easily adapted to this technique. Once sketched improvisationally and repeated in a mock-up of a quilt top, they often appear busy and disjointed. Sometimes they have potential to be reproduced on a large scale as an entire quilt design based on the single block. This idea is not illustrated in this book since we are focusing on the use of paper piecing for the purposes of repetition. If you are going to make a stand-alone large-scale block, it might be just as effective to piece improvisationally.

Figure 4

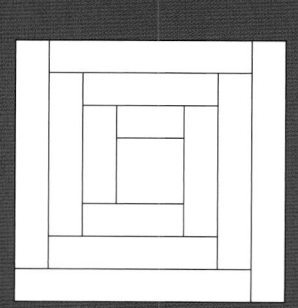

Figure 5

Tried-and-true traditional blocks provide a solid, comfortable springboard for creating new designs. If improvisation is outside of your comfort zone, working with traditional blocks will make you feel more at ease. Most quilters are familiar with improvisational versions of traditional blocks and easily recognize the aesthetic.

These blocks are based on the original, symmetrical, traditionally pieced, rotary-cut blocks, but they are constructed differently. They can be cut without the use of a straight edge and don't necessarily need to be measured.

tional-
ED

designs

# a little to THE LEFT

## The Exercise

The majority of traditional blocks are symmetrical. For this exercise, I encourage you to improvisationally sketch a traditional block so that it is no longer symmetrical (see left). This is a great starting point for beginners: you are taking a familiar block, but then playing with the lines a bit to create new intersections. For *Black Magic*, I introduced a new shape because I didn't begin the lines at the corners, which makes the block automatically asymmetrical. Remember, moving a little to the right in the pattern means the finished block will be a little to the left when pieced! Next, I played with the remaining diamond shapes within each of the quadrants, by varying the length and width of each diamond.

This quilt is made up of redesigned traditional Mill and Stars blocks, which are normally symmetrical. In the traditional block, the square is divided evenly by two diagonal lines that extend from corner to corner and cross in the center. I intended my block to be sewn in a similar manner, so I began my design with two offest diagonal lines. Then, within each section, I created a diamond shape with the addition of two lines per section. I did choose to make the diamond shapes meet at the seam lines of each section, but I varied the width and length of each diamond to create a truly asymmetrical block design.

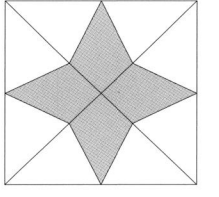
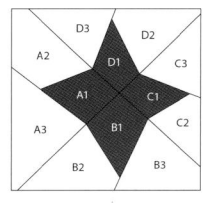

## Black Magic

**FINISHED BLOCK SIZE**
12˝ square

**FINISHED QUILT SIZE**
60˝ × 72˝

**NUMBER OF BLOCKS**
30

## Setting

When these blocks are placed together in a traditional row-and-column formation, the negative space creates unusual shapes. After arranging the blocks in a grid, I inverted many blocks and turned others on their sides. This adds variety and interest, and it's only apparent after looking at the quilt for a few moments that it is the same block being repeated. It appears that the blocks are improvised until you notice the repetition in both positive and negative spaces.

## Fabric and Quilting

I chose a palette of black and white because that simple contrast really shows off the shapes created by the pattern. For a dash of whimsy, I used an assortment of black and white prints that read as black.

The quilting is a diagonal crosshatch with irregularly spaced lines. The quilting adds a second improvisational design layer.

A pickle green for the binding adds an unexpected color to the black and white piecing. Again, incorporating the unexpected is part of the improv aesthetic. It can even extend to your choice of binding fabric!

## Materials List

Black Prints: approximately 30 fat eighths (one per block; may repeat selections)

Background Fabric: 7 yards (see the Tip on how to reduce the yardage requirement)

Backing Fabric: 4½ yards

Binding Fabric: ½ yard

Batting: 66″ × 78″

## PREPARATION

Print 30 copies of Templates A–D (see page 123).

> If some of your prints are directional, consider piecing some of your blocks with the intent of positioning them on their side or upside down as I did, so that the directionality is consistent. You do not want to piece all your blocks and then be limited to turning only those with non-directional prints.

## CUTTING

From each of the 30 black prints, cut:

(30) 6½″ × 4½″ rectangles (A1)
(30) 5″ × 6½″ rectangles (B1)
(30) 5½″ × 4″ rectangles (C1)
(30) 4″ × 6″ rectangles (D1)

From white solid background fabric, cut:
(30) 6½″ × 6¼″ (A2)
(30) 7½″ × 8″ (A3)
(30) 6″ × 7″ (B2)
(60) 6½″ × 6″ (B3, D2)
(30) 5″ × 5½″ (C2)
(30) 5½″ × 6″ (C3)
(30) 6½″ × 5½″ (D3)

> Working from 6½″ × WOF strips, without precutting but rather maximizing the angle cuts, saves significantly on yardage. Through careful piecing and cutting you should be able to get away with closer to 4 yards of background fabric. Note that the yardage for paper piecing varies greatly depending on your methods.

## ASSEMBLING THE BLOCK

**1.** Paper piece the sections, following the number order on the templates.

**2.** Sew Sections A to B. Press seams toward B.

**3.** Sew Sections C to D. Press seams toward D.

**4.** Sew AB and CD sets together. Press seams.

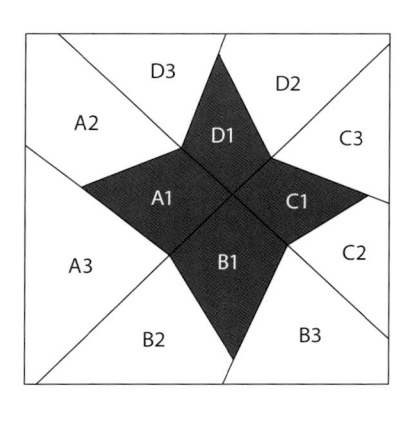

## ASSEMBLING THE QUILT TOP

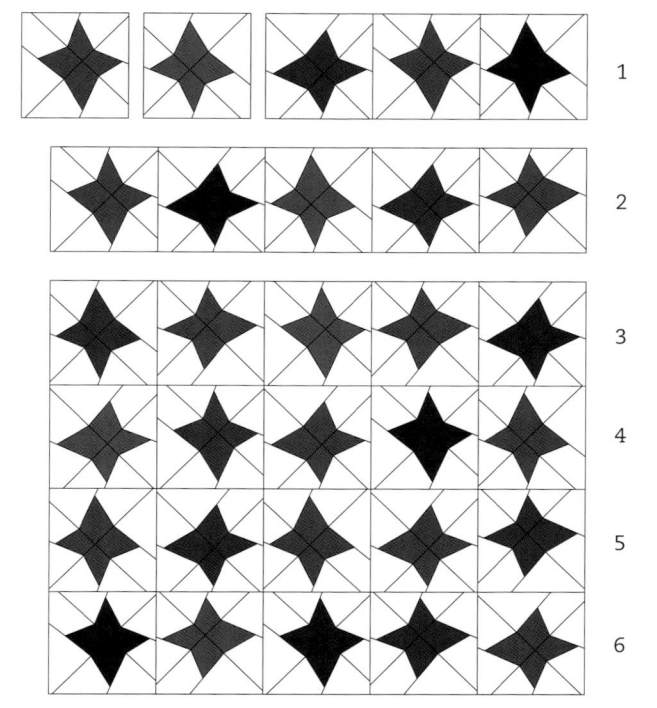

Construction Diagram

**1.** Arrange blocks in 6 rows of 5 blocks each, referencing the Construction Diagram. Alternate the directions of the blocks, inverting some and laying others on their 'sides'.

**2.** Sew the blocks into rows. Press the seams of odd-numbered rows to the right and even-numbered rows to the left.

**3.** Sew the rows together. All seams should nest nicely. Press.

## FINISHING

**1.** Layer quilt top with batting and backing fabric, then baste and quilt as desired.

**2.** Attach the binding using your favorite method.

# improv triangles

## The Exercise

Half-square triangles and quarter-square triangles are the building blocks of many traditional blocks. Rather than bisecting squares symmetrically from one corner point to one opposite corner point, try bisecting the block off-center. Pick a traditional block that includes either half-square triangles or quarter-square triangles and then try this exercise!

The traditional Hourglass block is a staple in the quilting world. It's also a simple block that's ideal for modification. An Hourglass is essentially a quarter-square triangle block. Each triangle is identical, made by extending lines from corner to corner, crossing at the center of a square. To make my improvisational Hourglass block, I began by creating two crossing diagonal lines. Rather than beginning at the corner of the block and crossing precisely at the center, I began with the lines shifted toward the center of the block a bit and let them cross where they may. It's not boldly different from the original, but the blocks no longer join in the same way. Then I added lines for "sand", playing off of the hourglass concept. Those lines were drawn so that they were not parallel with the top or bottom of the block.

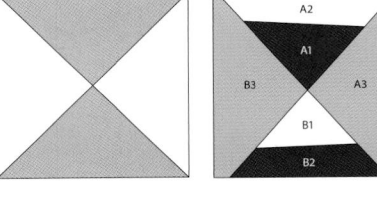

## Sixty Seconds

**FINISHED BLOCK SIZE**
8″ square

**FINISHED QUILT SIZE**
56″ × 64″

**NUMBER OF BLOCKS**
32; 16 blocks from original pattern, 16 from mirror image (invert half of each prior to piecing)

## Setting

When I began experimenting with arrangements for this block, it became clear that I needed to increase the negative space so that the composition wasn't too busy. I decided to base the design on the shape of the block: an hourglass. In order to add more of an improvisational feel to the quilt, I used a few variations of my initial sketch. I created 16 blocks from my original and 16 that were a mirror image of the original. Prior to piecing, I inverted half of each so that the fabric placement would be correct. The blocks were placed randomly into the hourglass layout and a few blocks were placed on their side.

## Fabric and Quilting

I kept the fabric selections simple so that the graphic shapes were the focus of the design. In keeping with the hourglass theme, though, I used black prints that were dotted or otherwise had the feel of falling sand. The whites were cut from a variety of tone-on-tone prints.

I chose to echo the hourglass shape with diagonal quilting lines in the solid background of the quilt. Within the "hourglass" created as a secondary pattern from the blocks, I quilted a crosshatch regular/irregular grid (see page 108). This means that I quilted parallel grid lines that were spaced one or two measured distances apart: some at ½" and some at 1".

## Materials List

**Assorted Black Prints:**
approximately 16 strips,
4″ × WOF

**Assorted White Prints:**
approximately 16 strips,
4″ × WOF

**Background Fabric:**
3 yards

**Backing Fabric: 4 yards**

**Binding Fabric: ½ yard**

**Batting: 62″ × 70″**

## PREPARATION

**1.** Make 16 copies of Templates A and B (see page 124) and 16 copies of Template C and D (see page 125). Invert half of each prior to piecing.

**2.** Mark the sections to be pieced in black with a black dot to avoid confusion while piecing.

## CUTTING

Option: Instead of cutting black and white prints as indicated below, work directly from 4″ strips (A1/B1) to minimize piecing waste (see page 21-22).

From black prints, cut:
   (32) 8½″ × 3″ rectangles (A2/B2)

From white prints, cut:
   (32) 8½″ × 3″ rectangles (A2/B2)

From the blue background fabric, cut:
   (11) 5½″ × WOF strips (A3/B3)
   • Work from this strip making economical use of the diagonal cut. You should be able to get 6 sections pieced from each WOF strip.
   (6) 8⅞″ squares
   • Bisect at the diagonal to make 12 triangles for negative-space piecing.
   (2) 24⅞″ squares
   • Bisect at the diagonal to make 4 triangles for negative-space piecing.

## ASSEMBLING THE BLOCK

1. Paper piece the sections, following the number order on the templates.

2. Sew Sections A to corresponding Sections B. Press seams to either side. Repeat for Sections C and D.

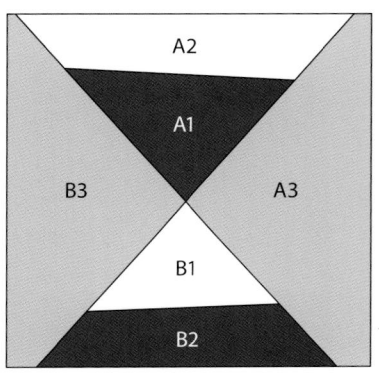

## ASSEMBLING THE QUILT TOP

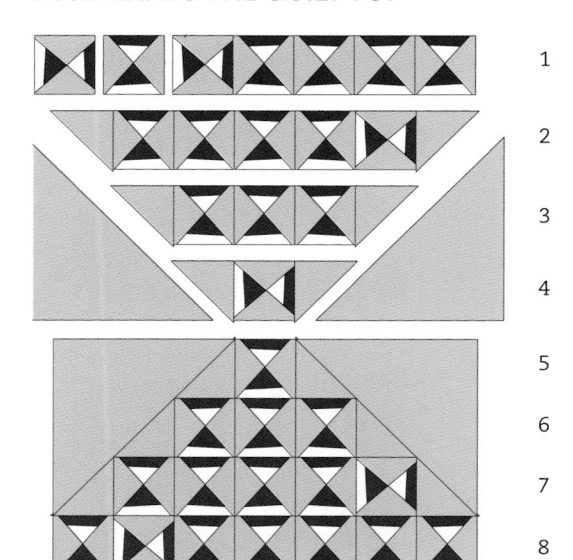

Construction Diagram

1. Place blocks in an hourglass shape, consulting the Construction Diagram. Randomly mix the types of blocks (original, mirror image, or inverted).

2. Sew the blocks together into rows. Press the seams of even-numbered rows to the right and odd-numbered rows to the left.

3. Sew triangles created by cutting the $8\frac{7}{8}''$ squares at the diagonal to both ends of Rows 2 through 7, consulting the Construction Diagram for directionality.

4. Sew Rows 2, 3, and 4 together. Press the seams down.

5. Sew Rows 5, 6, and 7 together. Press the seams down.

6. Sew the large triangles to assembled Rows 2–4 and assembled Rows 5–7. Press the seams toward the large triangles.

7. Sew these two sections together at the center seam.

8. Add Row 1 and Row 8.

## FINISHING

1. Layer the quilt top with batting and backing fabric, then baste and quilt as desired.

2. Attach the binding using your favorite method.

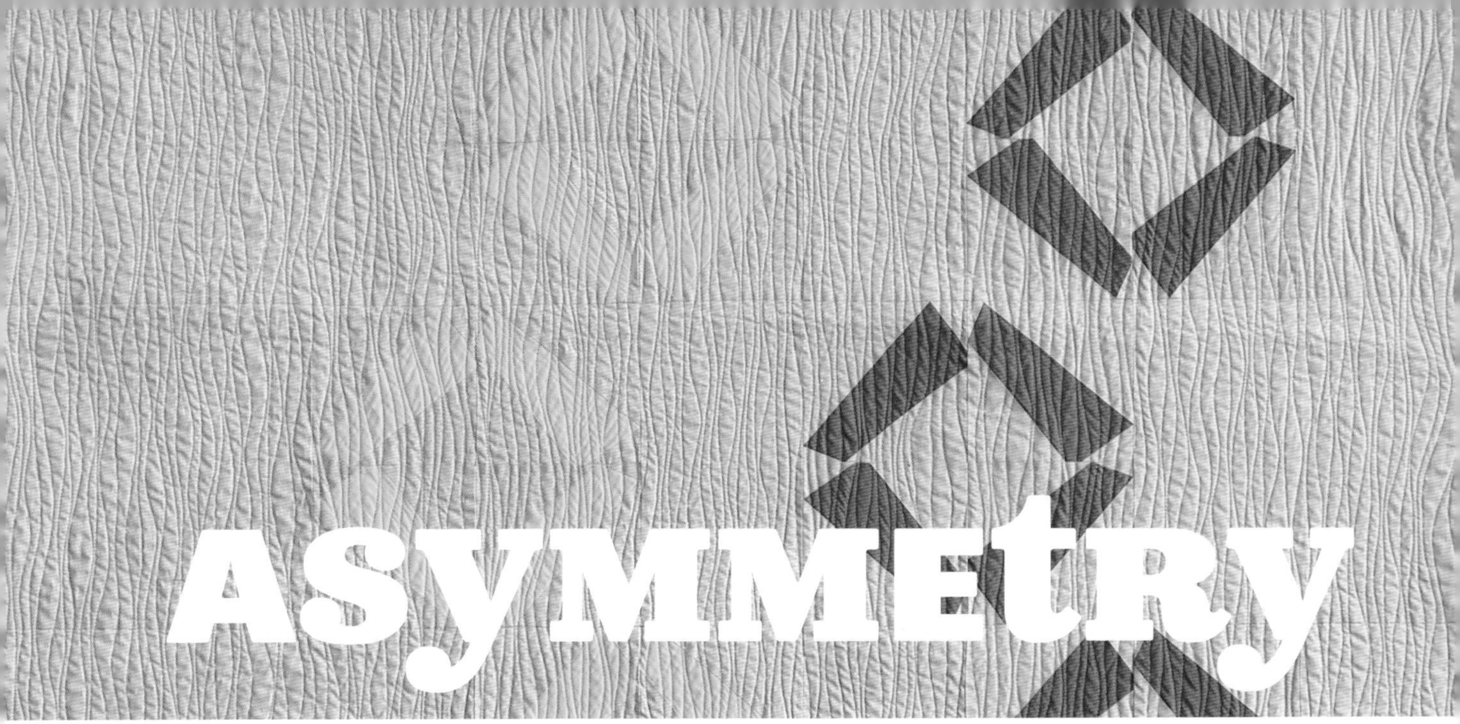

# ASYMMETRY

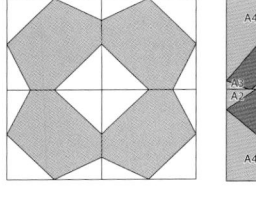 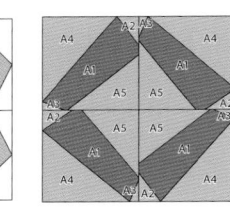

## Revolution

**FINISHED BLOCK SIZE**
6˝ quadrant, 12˝ square

**FINISHED QUILT SIZE**
60˝ × 72˝

**NUMBER OF BLOCKS**
48 quadrants, 12 blocks

## The Exercise

Symmetrical block designs tend to meet neighboring blocks at perfect points along the seam lines. This often creates interesting secondary designs, but the patterns also tend to feel expected and predictable. In this exercise, we'll modify a traditional block so that it is no longer symmetrical and the shapes will not meet at the seam lines; this often leads to a more unexpected and dynamic design. Try modifying a traditional block that has identical quadrants and see how the blocks play with each other along the seam lines. Keep the quadrants identical, but watch the seam intersections. Do you like what you see? Can you turn the quadrants or add a mirror image of the quadrant to make it work?

*Revolution* is based on the traditional Tallahassee block. As you can see from the original, each quadrant is symmetrical in and of itself. In order to create a fresh block based on this one, I drew lines so that the design within the quadrant is no longer symmetrical; it is narrower at one end and wider at the other, making the inner and outer triangles of background color asymmetrical as well. You will see that the quadrants no longer match at the seams either. The new design created by positioning the quadrants in a "narrow-edge-to-wider-edge" configuration feels a bit like the block is spinning, which I like!

## Setting

I played with different arrangements of this block and found that what I liked best was a design that echoes the sense of motion in the block. I positioned the blocks in a sort of serpentine fashion, incorporating negative space. See page 96 where I auditioned a few different setting styles with this block. I ended up using an alternate gridwork in order to reinforce the feeling of movement created in each completed block.

## Fabric and Quilting

I used solids. I auditioned gradients and prints but they didn't have the same impact. The limited palette of solids contributes to the clean overall design. A fourth color was used for the binding as a way of sneaking another color into the palette, and it's in keeping with the practice of embracing the unexpected.

I quilted vertical wavy lines using my walking foot. My reasoning was twofold. First, it echoes the serpentine layout of the blocks. Second, they mask the pieced seams, which detract from the impact of the composition. I didn't want the viewer to notice the details of the construction, just the design.

## Materials List:

**Lime Green Fabric:** ⅔ yard

**Violet Fabric:** ⅔ yard

**Background Fabric: 4 yards**

**Backing Fabric: 4½ yards**

**Binding Fabric: ½ yard**

**Batting: 66″ × 78″**

## PREPARATION

Print 48 copies of *Revolution* Template (see page 126).

## CUTTING

From both the lime green and the violet fabrics, cut:

(24) 3½″ × 8½″ rectangles (A1)

From the lavender background fabric, cut:
(24) 3″ × 3½″ rectangles
- Bisect at diagonal to create 48 triangles (A2)

(24) 2″ × 3″ rectangles
- Bisect at diagonal to create 48 triangles (A3)

(24) 7″ squares
- Bisect at diagonal to create 48 triangles (A4)

(24) 5½″ × 7″ rectangles
- Bisect at diagonal to create 48 triangles (A5)

For the negative space blocks, from the background fabric, cut:
(6) 12½″ × WOF strips
- From the first strip, subcut: (2) 18½″ and (1) 6½″ units
- From the second strip, subcut: (1) 12½″, (1) 24½″ and (1) 6½″ units
- From third strip, subcut: (2) 6½″, (1) 12½″ and (1) 18½″ untis
- From the fourth strip, subcut: (2) 12½″ and (2) 6½″ units
- From the fifth strip, subcut: (1) 18½″ and (1) 24½″units
- From the final strip, subcut: (2) 6½″ units

## ASSEMBLING THE BLOCK

1. Referencing the Block Diagram below, paper piece the sections, following the number order on the templates. Repeat to create 4 units of the same colors.

2. Arrange the block (Fig. 1). Stitch the two upper quadrants together, right sides facing. Repeat for the remaining two quadrants.

3. Press the seams in opposite directions so that they nest. Stitch the center seam. Do not press the center seam at this point.

4. Repeat to create a total of 6 blocks in lime and 6 in violet.

## ASSEMBLING THE QUILT TOP

1. In each row, sew the units together from left to right.

   **ROW 1:** Sew one 18½˝ × 12½˝ rectangle of background fabric to one lime block, to one 6½˝ × 12½˝ rectangle of background fabric, to one violet block, to one 12½˝ square of background fabric.

   **ROW 2:** Sew one 24½˝ × 12½˝ rectangle of background fabric to one lime block, to one 6½˝ × 12½˝ rectangle of background fabric, to one violet block, to another 6½˝ × 12½˝ rectangle of background fabric.

   **ROW 3:** Repeat directions for Row 1.

   **ROW 4:** Sew one 12½˝ square of background fabric to one lime block, to one 6½˝ × 12½˝ rectangle, to one violet block, to one 18½˝ × 12½˝ rectangle of background fabric.

   **ROW 5:** Repeat directions for Row 1.

   **ROW 6:** Repeat directions for Row 2.

2. Press the seams of odd numbered rows to the right and even numbered rows to the left.

3. Sew the rows together. All seams should nest nicely. Press.

## FINISHING

1. Layer the quilt top with the batting and backing fabric, then baste and quilt as desired.

2. Attach the binding using your favorite method.

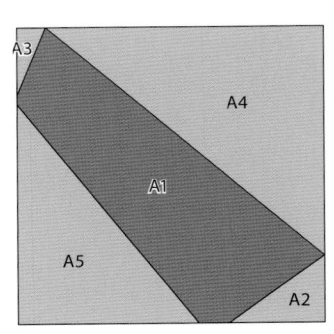

Block Diagram

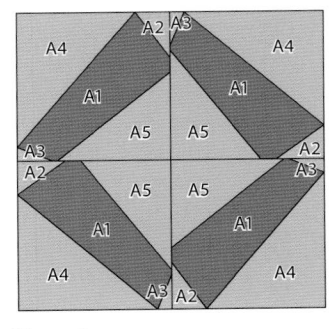

Figure 1

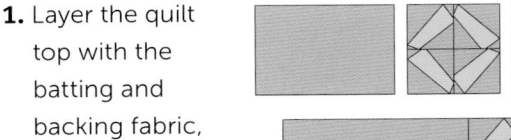

1

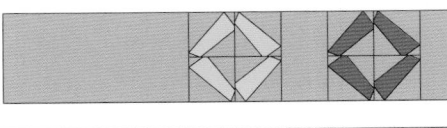

2

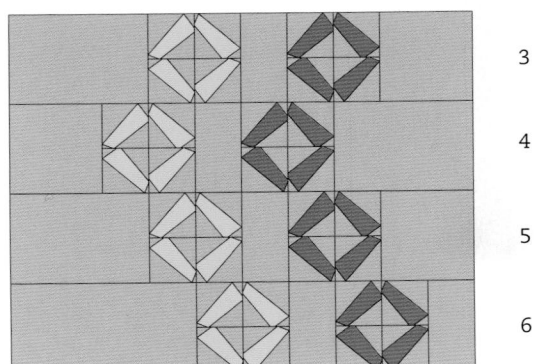

3

4

5

6

Construction Diagram

intro to shaba

A shape-based process yields surprising results. Try beginning with a well-defined, symmetrical shape, such as a diamond or square, and then breaking up the space with randomly placed lines. The lines could radiate from a corner or crisscross back and forth, creating wedges. They could be arranged in a crazy quilt or Log Cabin style. These lines are straight so that they can be paper pieced, but they are not measured or equidistant. This process has so many variations that can be explored and different approaches are illustrated in each of the quilts shared here. One quilt design begins with a symmetrical shape broken up improvisationally as described above. The possibilities are endless!

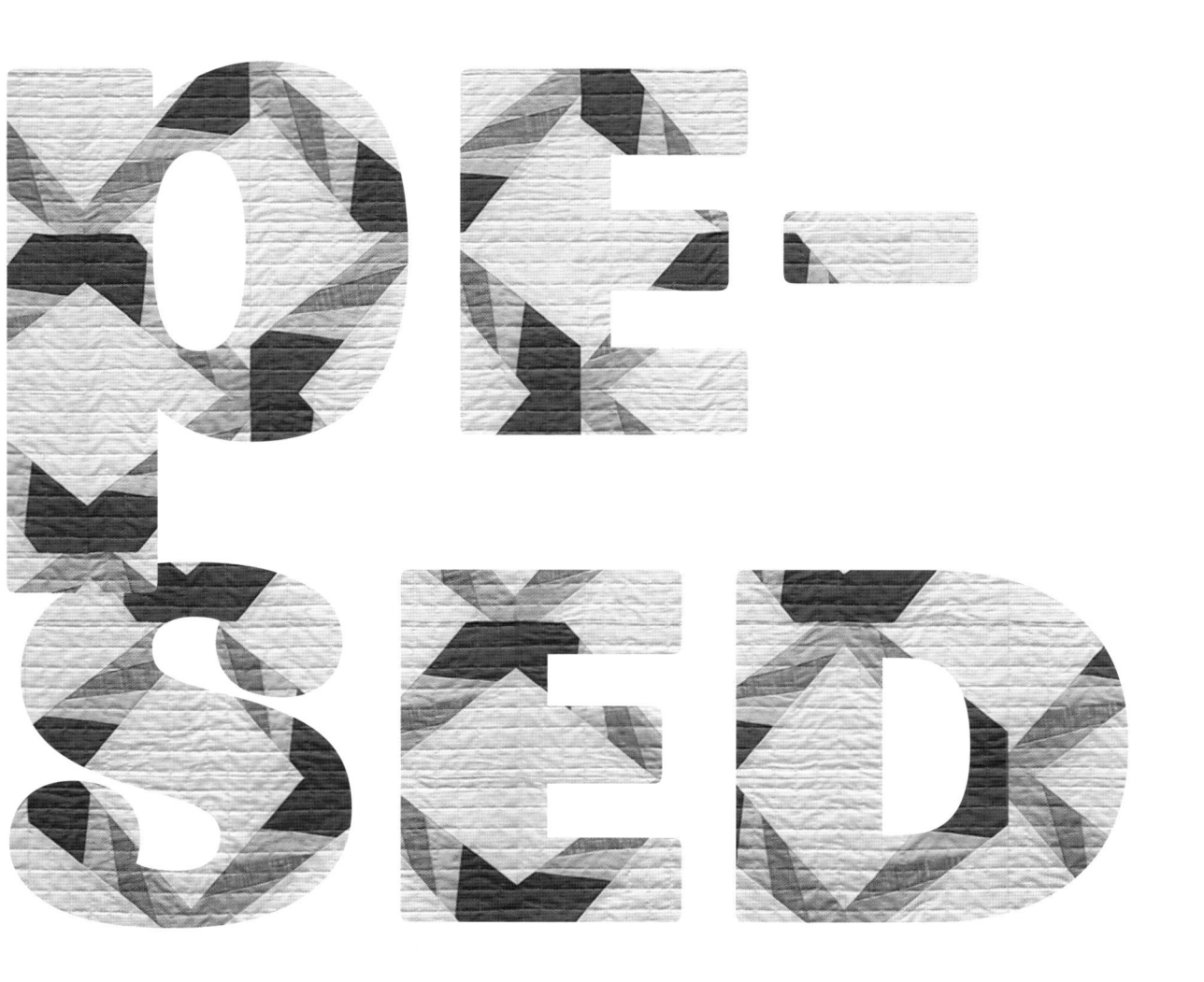

# PE-
# SED
*designs*

# SyMMetry

## The Exercise

There are many ways to approach a shape-based design. For this exercise, begin with a symmetrical shape of your choice: a square, a rectangle, an equilateral triangle, a diamond, etc. In *Peacock Crossing*, I used a simple wedge. Then, break up the space within the shape with quick, freehand-drawn lines that may be quickly sketched in a matter of seconds. Your initial shape can either be drawn within a traditional square block (like an equilateral triangle inside of a square block) or it can be your building block. For example, you could use an isosceles triangle or a hexagon shape alone and sew them together.

*Peacock Crossing* illustrates the most straightforward approach to design based on an initial geometric shape. If you really allow your hand to divide the space within your shape freely, your lines will appear a bit askew and the resulting spaces between sections are interesting and quirky. Resist the temptation to readjust and make these lines parallel.

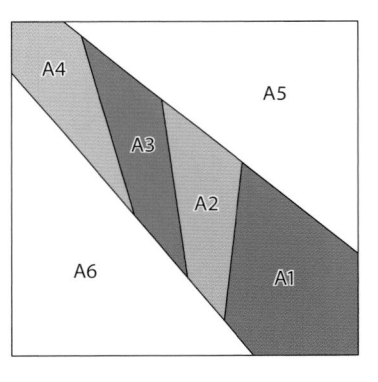

## Peacock Crossing

FINISHED BLOCK SIZE
8˝ square

FINISHED QUILT SIZE
64˝ × 64˝

NUMBER OF BLOCKS
64

## Setting

I arranged the blocks into several formations. Many of them still looked too structured for this exercise until I rearranged them into a crisscrossing formation. Here they have a pattern, yet it isn't where matching pieces meet and line up as expected. As a result, the design has a new energy. (For more, see Layout section on page 92.)

## Fabric and Quilting

Once my block was sketched, I thought it looked a bit like a feather so I went with a peacock palette. I used mostly solids and one print that reads as a solid to draw the eye across the quilt.

The quilting is an evenly spaced grid. Sometimes superimposing a regular grid on an asymmetrical design provides a nice contrast.

## Materials List:

**Royal Blue Fabric:** 1¼ yards

**Medium Pink Fabric:** 1 yard

**Pickle Green Fabric:** 1 yard

**Light Blue Fabric:** 1 yard

**Background Fabric:** 3½ yards

**Backing Fabric:** 4 yards

**Binding Fabric:** ½ yard

**Batting:** 70″ × 70″

## PREPARATION

Print 64 copies of *Peacock Crossing* Template (see page 127).

## CUTTING

From the royal blue fabric, cut:

(64) 4″ × 5½″ rectangles (A1)

From the medium pink fabric, cut:
(64) 3″ × 6″ rectangles (A2)

From the pickle green fabric, cut:
(64) 2½″ × 7″ rectangles (A3)

From the light blue fabric, cut:
(64) 3″ × 6″ rectangles (A4)

From the light pink background fabric, cut:
(64) 9″ × 7¾″ rectangles
  • Bisect along the diagonal to create 128 triangles (A5, A6)

## ASSEMBLING THE BLOCK

Assemble 64 blocks following the piecing diagram order indicated on the pattern.

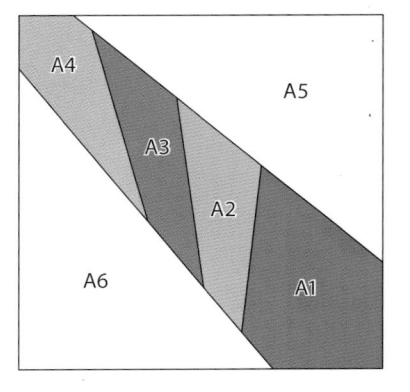

## ASSEMBLING THE QUILT TOP

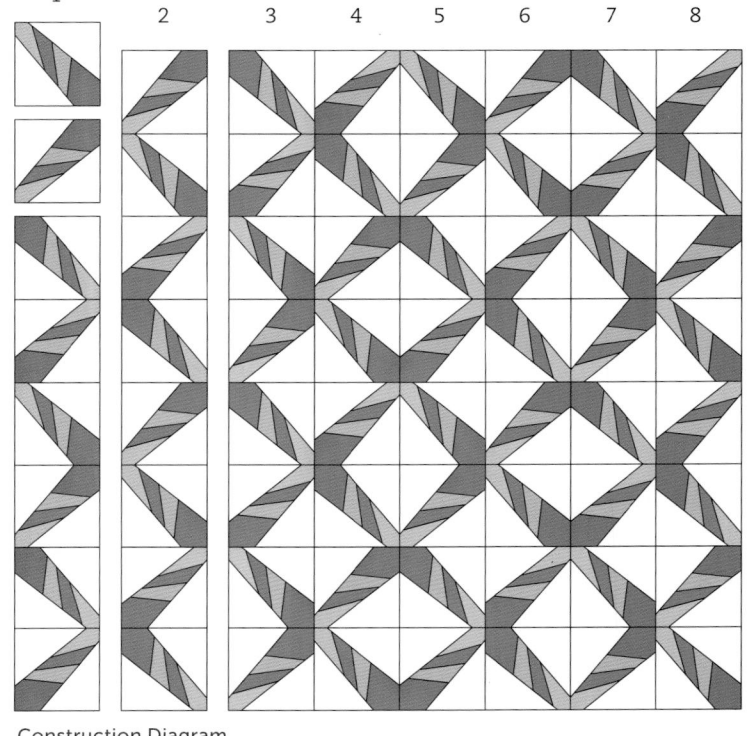

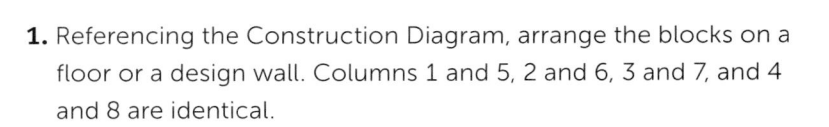

Construction Diagram

1. Referencing the Construction Diagram, arrange the blocks on a floor or a design wall. Columns 1 and 5, 2 and 6, 3 and 7, and 4 and 8 are identical.

2. Sew the blocks into columns.

3. Press seams of odd-numbered columns down and even-numbered columns up.

4. Sew the columns together. All seams should nest nicely. Press.

## FINISHING

1. Layer the quilt top with batting and backing fabric, then baste and quilt as desired.

2. Attach the binding using your favorite method.

# scale

## The Exercise

For this exercise, we will play with scale and irregular sashing. Begin with a shape that is either symmetrical or irregular. Play with scale by making two blocks using that same shape—one larger and one smaller within the same size finished block. Place the shapes within the block using irregular sashing or placement. When the blocks are sewn together, the irregular sashing or the placement, combined with the rotation of the blocks, leads to a random, scattered appearance in the final layout.

The beginning shape for this design is the square. I decided to experiment with scale and created two blocks, one a larger square and one a small square. Both squares are just that—square, complete with 90-degree angles and equal-length sides. But I decided to place them within larger blocks and use widths of uneven sashing. The space within the square is divided up haphazardly with a crazy-quilt feel. If you are new to paper piecing, you may notice that by employing this traditional aesthetic, it makes the process of paper piecing feel more comfortable to you.

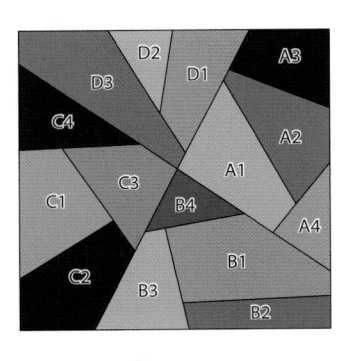

## Sea Glass

**FINISHED BLOCK SIZE**
12″ square

**FINISHED QUILT SIZE**
51″ × 68″

**NUMBER OF BLOCKS**
3 large blocks, 8 small blocks

Quilting by Christina Lane, The Sometimes Crafter

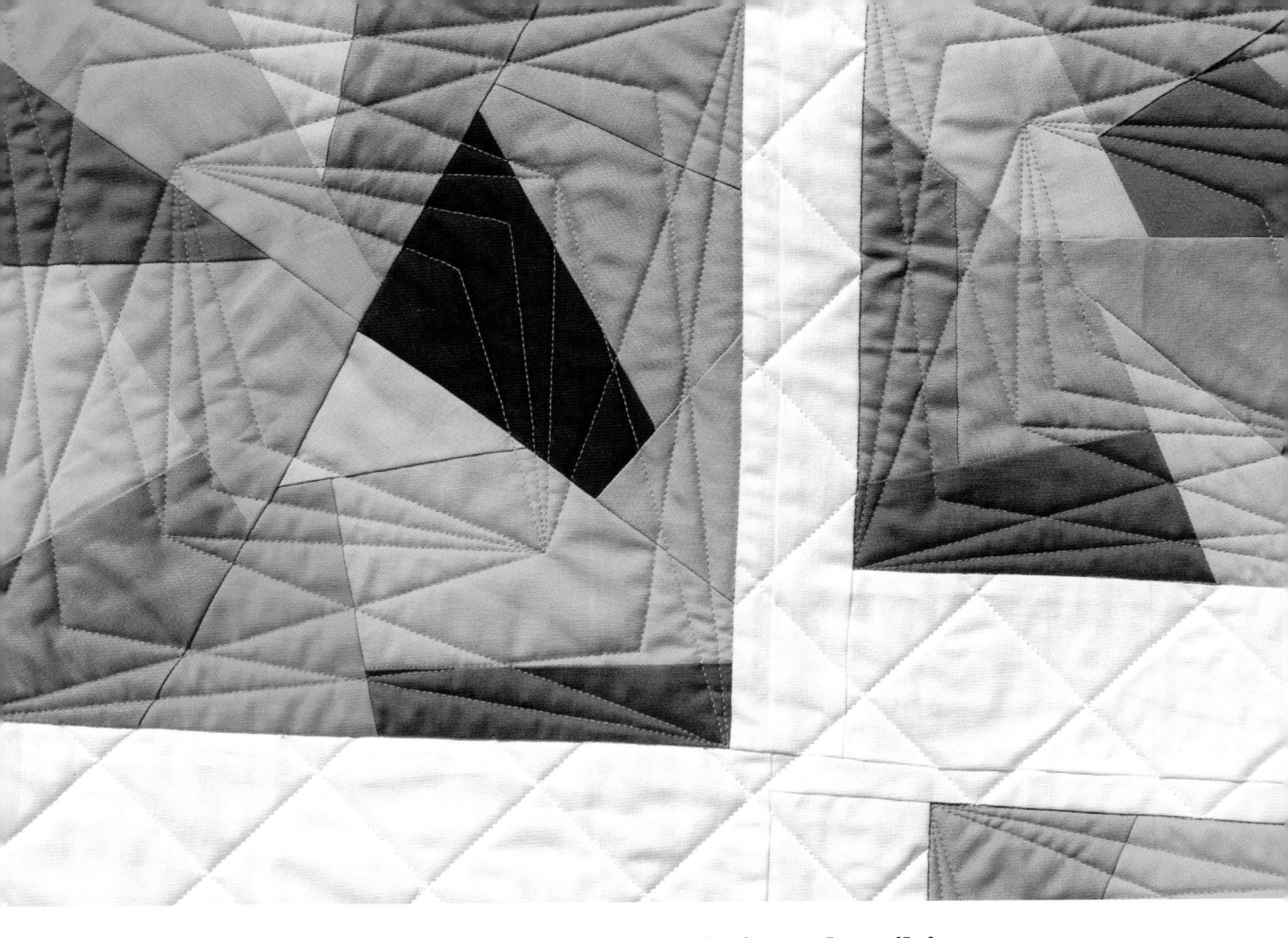

## Setting

The blocks are arranged on-point in a pattern, but some of the blocks are turned to the side or inverted so that the uneven sashing creates an interesting scattering. There are a couple of dominant shapes within the crazy-quilt–like space that catch the eye.

They encourage the viewer to explore the quilt top and to identify the shape in each block, though they may be twisted and turned. Play around with arranging your blocks too, based on the contrast you create in each.

## Fabric and Quilting

The lines and color palette of this quilt are inspired by sea-tossed and smoothed sea glass found on the beach. Once again, the use of solids focuses the eye on the shapes created by the piecing.

This quilt has a lot of negative space and I asked Christina Lane to work her long-arm quilting magic on it. She worked with the theme and created a zigzag edge as a graphic way of representing the water washing on the shore with circular bubbles for foam. The quilting inside the squares suggests the prismatic quality of glass shards, while the grid is a representation of the sand grains.

## Materials List

**Sea-Glass–Inspired Solids:** approximately 11 fat quarters ranging from light blues and mint, through to navy.

**Background Fabric:** 3¼ yards

**Backing Fabric:** 4 yards

**Binding Fabric:** ½ yard

**Batting:** 57˝ × 74˝

### PREPARATION

Print 3 sets of pattern pieces for the Large Block (see page 128).

Print 8 sets of pattern pieces for the Small Block (see page 129).

### CUTTING

From the white background fabric, cut:

for the Large Blocks:
- (3) 2˝ × 12½˝ strips
- (3) 2½˝ × 10½˝ strips
- (3) 1˝ × 12½˝ strips

for the Small Blocks:
- (8) 2˝ × 8½˝ strips
- (8) 3½˝ × 12½˝ strips
- (8) 3˝ × 8½˝ strips
- (8) 1½˝ × 12½˝ strips

for the Negative Space:
- (3) 12½˝ × 24½˝ rectangles
- (1) 12½˝ square

for the Setting Triangles:
- (3) 18¼˝ squares
  Subcut twice on diagonal but discard 2 triangles

for the Corner Triangles:
- (2) 9⅜˝ squares
  Subcut once on diagonal

Selecting colors randomly but somewhat equally from the sea-glass-inspired solids, cut:

for the Large Blocks:
- (9) 4½˝ × 6½˝ units (A1, A2, B1)
- (9) 3½˝ × 4½˝ units (A3, A4, D2)
- (3) 2½˝ × 6˝ units (B2)
- (6) 4½˝ squares (B3, C1)
- (3) 3˝ × 4½˝ units (B4)
- (12) 4˝ × 5½˝ units (C2, C3, C4, D1)
- (3) 4˝ × 8½˝ units (D3)

for the Small Blocks:
- (8) 3½˝ × 4½˝ units (A1)
- (8) 2½˝ × 6½˝ units (A2)
- (8) 3˝ × 5½˝ units (A3)
- (8) 4˝ × 6˝ units (A4)
- (8) 3˝ × 3½˝ units (B1)
- (8) 4˝ squares (B2)
- (8) 4˝ × 5˝ units (B3)
- (8) 4½˝ squares (C1)
- (8) 3½˝ × 5˝ units (C2, C3)
- (8) 3½˝ × 6˝ units (C4)

Large Block

Small Block

## ASSEMBLING THE BLOCK

**1.** Paper piece and assemble 3 Large Blocks.

**2.** Sew Section A to Section B. Press seams toward B.

**3.** Sew Section C to Section D. Press seams toward D.

**4.** Sew AB and CD sets together. Press the seam.

**5.** With the right sides facing, stitch one $10\frac{1}{2}'' \times 2\frac{1}{2}''$ strip of white background fabric to the top. Press. With the right sides together, stitch one $2'' \times 12\frac{1}{2}''$ strip of background fabric to the left side and one $1'' \times 12\frac{1}{2}''$ strip to the right side. Press.

**6.** Paper piece and assemble 8 Small Blocks.

**7.** Sew Section B to Section C. Press seam toward B.

**8.** Sew BC to Section A. Press the seam.

**9.** With the right sides together, stitch one $1\frac{1}{2}'' \times 8\frac{1}{2}''$ strip of background fabric to the left side and one $3'' \times 8\frac{1}{2}''$ strip to the right side. Press. Next, with the right sides facing, sew a strip $12\frac{1}{2}'' \times 3\frac{1}{2}''$ to the top and $12\frac{1}{2}'' \times 1\frac{1}{2}''$ to the bottom. Press.

## ASSEMBLING THE QUILT TOP

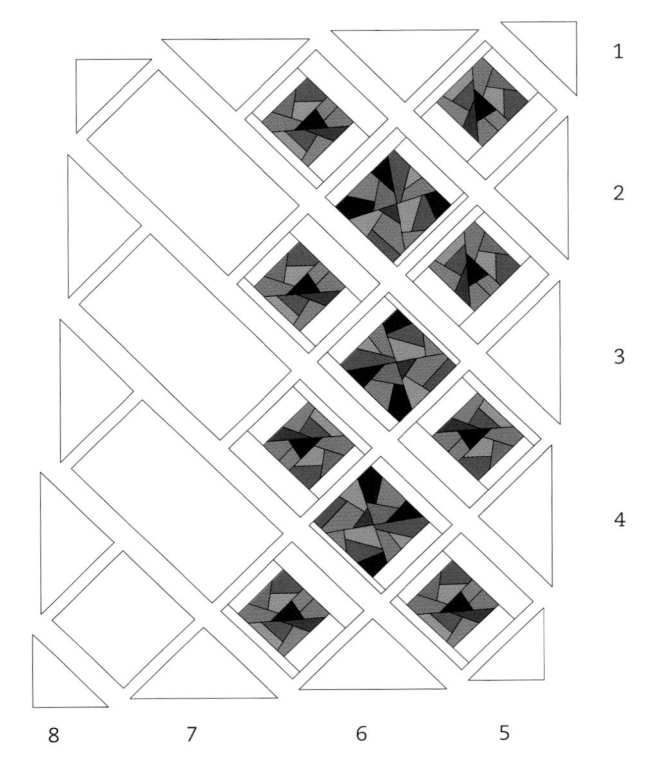

Construction Diagram

**1.** Referencing the Construction Diagram, arrange the Negative Space Blocks, Setting Triangles and Corner Triangles.

**2.** Sew the blocks together into diagonal columns.

**3.** Press the seams of odd-numbered columns down and even-numbered columns up.

**4.** Sew the columns together. All seams should nest nicely. Press.

## FINISHING

**1.** Layer the quilt top with the batting and the backing fabric, then baste and quilt as desired.

**2.** Attach the binding using your favorite method.

# wonky

## The Exercise

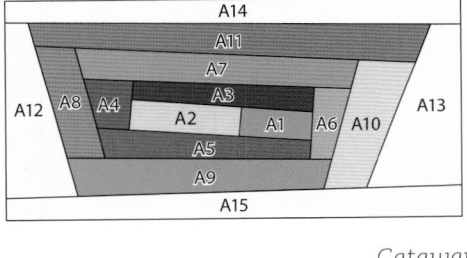

Rather than beginning with a symmetrical shape, in this exercise I'd like you to begin by improvisationally sketching a shape and leaving it irregular. In this case, the shape I sketched was a very wonky half-hexagon. Now, break up the interior space in your template with improv divisions.

## Catawampus

**FINISHED BLOCK SIZE**
16˝ × 8˝

**FINISHED QUILT SIZE**
64˝ × 64˝

**NUMBER OF BLOCKS**
32 total, 16 of each

*Catawampus* is a word that can be used to describe something that is out of alignment or crooked. I began my design with the half-hexagon shape. Rather than drawing the initial shape symmetrically, I decided to draw exaggerated lines that were askew so that the hexagon shape was crooked. Then I began to break up the space within. I used the traditional Log Cabin construction technique, but once again created lines that were not parallel or measured. Using this familiar traditional technique of construction, but then just modifying it slightly by using irregularly shaped strips instead of the traditional even-width strips, makes the improvisational paper piecing designs more approachable, for those who are new to the process.

## Setting

After considering some possible block arrangements using just the first block I drafted, I decided to make a second block pattern to pair with the first so that I would be creating a broken hexagon. I repeated the same design process to create the second block, then I arranged the blocks in pairs. Staggering the rows created great energy. Notice the "zigzag-y" movement in the negative space between the columns.

## Fabric and Quilting

I made a test block using a number of prints and found that it was too busy, distracting the eye from the improvisational-looking shapes within the block. So I decided to make the blocks from solids, using no more than a few prints per block.

The seam lines of the blocks, along with the elongated half-hexagon shapes, are both strong horizontal features. I love the effect the hexagons have in this setting, almost as if they are falling. Wanting to accentuate that verticality, I quilted with evenly spaced vertical lines.

## Materials List

**Assortment of scraps ranging from 2″ to 3″ wide in various lengths**

I used a color palette inspired by fall leaves and flowers, including deep red, burnt orange, gold, yellow, rust, purple, lavender, and pink.

**Background Fabric: 3½ yards**

**Backing Fabric: 4 yards**

**Binding Fabric: ½ yard**

**Batting: 70″ × 70″**

## PREPARATION

Print 16 copies of Template A, Block A and 16 copies of Template B, Block B (see pages 130 and 131).

From the soft yellow background fabric, cut:
  (16) 2″ × WOF strips (A14, A15)
  (12) 7″ × WOF strips (A12, A13), cut as needed

Working from WOF strips without precutting but rather maximizing the angle cuts (see pages 21-22), saves significantly on yardage.

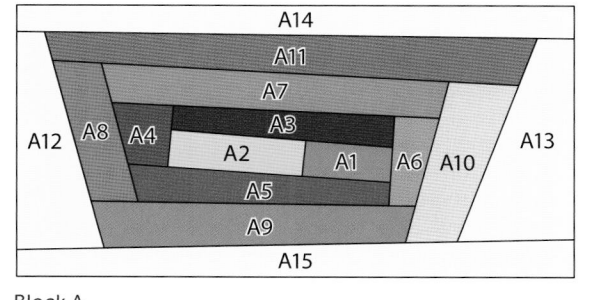

Block A

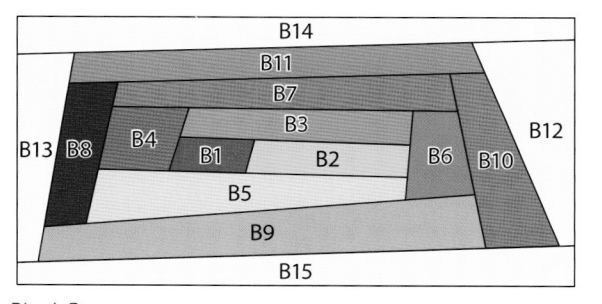

Block B

## ASSEMBLING THE BLOCK

Assemble 16 of Block A and 16 of Block B, for a total of 32.

## ASSEMBLING THE QUILT TOP

Construction Diagram

1. Referencing the Construction Diagram, arrange the blocks into 8 rows of 4 blocks each. Alternate Block A and B, and play with inverting some of your blocks until you find a composition you like. Rows 1, 3, 5, and 7 are identical, as are Rows 2, 4, 6 and 8.

2. Sew the blocks into rows.

3. Press the seams of odd-numbered Rows down and the seams of even-numbered Rows up.

4. Sew the rows together. All seams should nest nicely. Press.

## FINISHING

1. Layer the quilt top with the batting and the backing fabric, then baste and quilt as desired.

2. Attach the binding using your favorite method.

A simple object can serve as inspiration for a block design too. Keep an eye out for objects with few components, strong lines, and simple shapes. For example, an evergreen tree can be broken into a triangle for the greens and a rectangle for the trunk. Starting with an object made at least mostly of straight lines, will also make the piecing process easier. Look at the object, break it into its simplest graphic form, and sketch it improvisationally. Don't worry if the result doesn't resemble the inspiration: it doesn't matter. The inspiration has already served its purpose when you have completed your sketch.

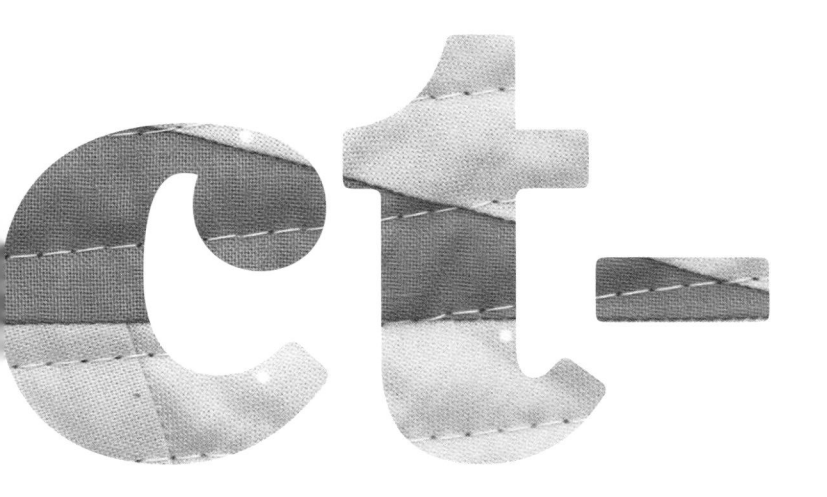

*designs*

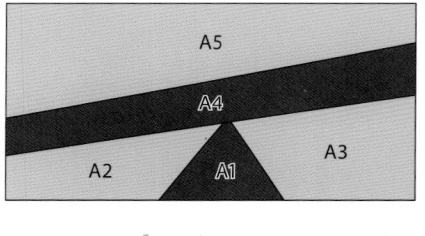

## The Exercise

Find a sign and use it as your inspiration for this exercise. You can find signs in your everyday environment. If you keep your eyes open, you will be surprised at just how many there are to choose from. You can also search online using the term "traffic and street sign images." Starting with a great inspirational image will help you to be successful. Look for simple signage with bold graphics, but release yourself from the expectation that your block design will bear a strong likeness to the sign. It is only serving as inspiration.

Simple signage is a treasure trove of inspiration for block designs. I noticed a seesaw symbol used to indicate a playground, and just like that I found my inspiration.

When I improvisationally sketched my pattern, I set my triangle slightly off-center. I quickly set the slant of the seesaw without measuring and varied the width of the board as it went from left to right. The lower line cut off the tip of my triangle, and that's just how I left it.

### Upsetting the Balance

FINISHED BLOCK SIZE
12˝ × 6˝

FINISHED QUILT SIZE
60˝ × 60˝

NUMBER OF BLOCKS
50

## Setting

I chose to use both the original block and its mirror image to create the setting. By using the mirror image, I could create a chevron design that accentuated the seesaw board's subtle variation in width. About two thirds of the way down the quilt, I turned the blocks upside down and shifted the chevron pattern, "upsetting the balance." The unexpected is often a byproduct of improvisation but can also be the result of modern design choices. Trust me, it works!

## Fabric and Quilting

Rather than using solids for this quilt, I chose all navy prints. The prints are mostly tonal so they work like solids in that they help keep the design cohesive, but add interest. I chose a bold, nearly complementary color, for the background for contrast. Bold color choices are also a modern quilting characteristic.

The quilting breaks partway down the quilt, complementing the break in the block pattern. The quilted lines are evenly spaced and vertical for the top two thirds of the quilt. The bottom portion is quilted in a chevron pattern, mimicking the angle of the piecing.

## Materials List

**Assorted Blue Prints:
2 yards total**

**Background Fabric: 4½ yards**

**Backing Fabric: 3¾ yards**

**Binding Fabric: ½ yard**

**Batting: 66˝ × 66˝**

## PREPARATION

Print 29 copies of Template A, Block A and 21 copies of Template B, Block B (see pages 132 and 133).

## CUTTING

From the blue prints, cut:
  (50) 4½˝ × 3½˝ rectangles (A1)
  (50) 14˝ × 2½˝ strips (A4)

From the gold background fabric, cut:
  (10) 3½˝ × WOF strips
    • Subcut into (50) 3½˝ × 8˝ rectangles (A2)
  (9) 4½˝ × WOF strips
    • Subcut into (50) 4½˝ × 7˝ rectangles (A3)
  (9) 8˝ × WOF strips
    • Subcut into (25) 8˝ × 14˝ rectangles then subcut each diagonally with a ruler placed 5˝ down from the upper left corner and 3˝ down from the upper right corner to create 50 pieces (A5)

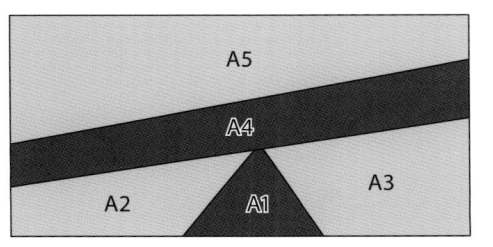

Block A

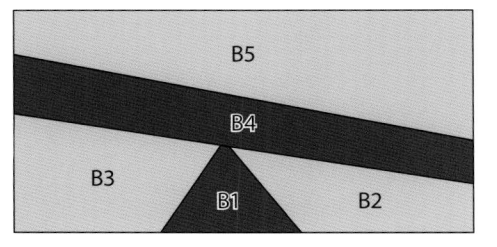

Block B

## ASSEMBLING THE BLOCK

Assemble 29 of Block A and 21 of Block B for a total of 50 blocks. Follow the piecing order indicated on the patterns.

## ASSEMBLING THE QUILT TOP

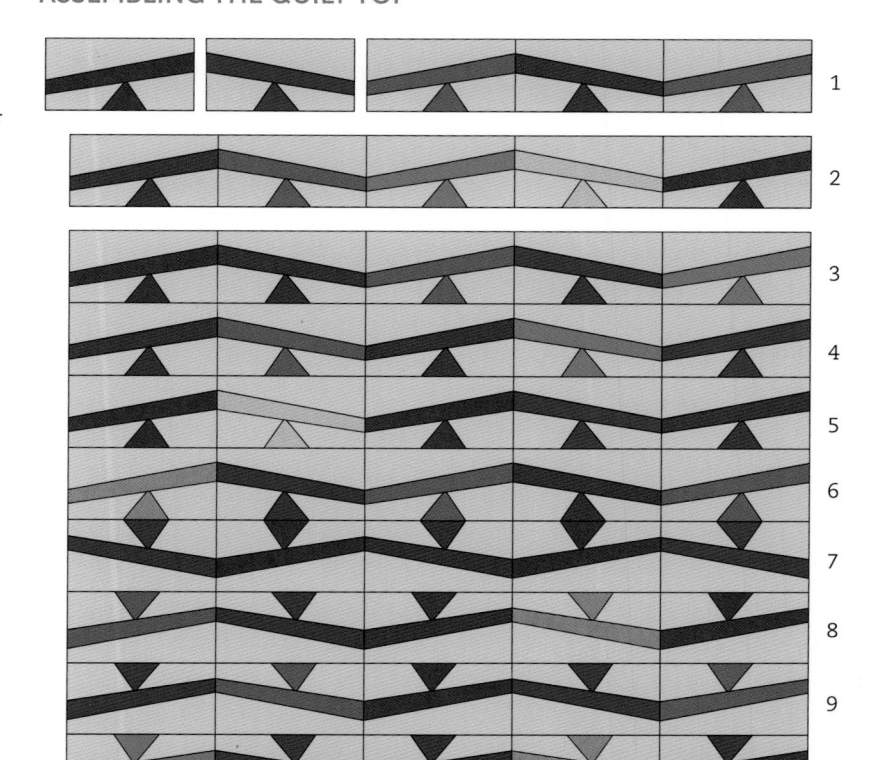

Construction Diagram

1. Arrange the blocks into 10 rows of 5 blocks each by referencing the Construction Diagram. Rows 1–6 are identical. Rows 8–10 are also identical, but they are placed upside down on your design wall or large surface.

2. Sew the blocks into rows.

3. Press the seams of odd-numbered rows to the right and even-numbered rows to the left.

4. Sew the rows together. All seams should nest nicely. Press.

## FINISHING

1. Layer the quilt top with the batting and backing fabric, then baste and quilt as desired.

2. Attach the binding using your favorite method.

# architecture

## The Exercise

### Paper Trail

**FINISHED BLOCK SIZE**
16˝ × 12˝

**FINISHED QUILT SIZE**
64˝ × 72˝

**NUMBER OF BLOCKS**
24

Architecture is a fantastic source of inspiration for designs. Many buildings tend to be angular, which is perfect for our purposes since we want to create straight-line designs. Find an inspirational image and break it down into the simplest shapes possible, ignoring minor details like trim. Or, focus only on one detail like an architectural ornament, break it down into a simple form and improvisationally sketch that form. Remember, you are simply using the inspiration to give you an idea of what to create, not attempting to replicate the inspiration image exactly.

The inspiration for this design was a step pyramid, of all things. What can I say? I have grade-school children and happened to have an Egyptian project going on at home at the time. This only goes to prove that inspiration is all around you: you just need to look!

I created the horizontal lines without measuring and intentionally skewed the lines so that they were not parallel. I also made sure that the width between the lines varied in height. Then I created the "steps" with the addition of vertical lines, which I also took care to skew. The resulting block design could just as easily have been inspired by a layered cake or a bee skep, but the step pyramid provided the design prompt and the end result isn't expected to be a replica of that inspirational shape.

## Settings

After I designed this block, I started playing with possible settings. When I hit upon this one, I knew immediately that this was it! I loved how the blocks created an almost twisting design which is actually quite a departure from the pyramid shape that inspired the original block design. See the Layout section on page 98 for more information on how I settled on this final setting for the quilt.

## Fabric and Quilting

I mocked up this design in so many color options and really loved all of them. It's a versatile pattern and a good use for whatever you have the most of in your stash. I have (or, should I say, had) a lot of low volume prints, so that's what swayed me. I paired them with a cinnamon solid.

This quilt has a lot of seams, and I will confess that I sometimes find seams beautiful. This is one of those times. I decided to quilt rather sparsely, mimicking the angles of the seam lines back and forth within each column. The seam lines became my quilting inspiration.

## Materials List

**Low Volume Fabric: 50 strips, 3″ × WOF from as many prints as you wish**

**Background Fabric: 4½ yards**

**Backing Fabric: 4½ yards**

**Binding Fabric: ½ yard**

**Batting: 70″ × 78″**

## PREPARATION

Print 24 copies of Templates A-G (see page 134-135).

## CUTTING

From the low volume fabric, cut:
  (50) 3″ × WOF strips (A1, B1, C1, D1, E1, F1, G1)

From the cinnamon background fabric, cut:
  (30) 3″ × WOF strips (A2, A3, B3, C2, D2, E3, F2, G2, G3)
  (18) 3¾″ × WOF strips (B2, C3, D3, E2, F3)

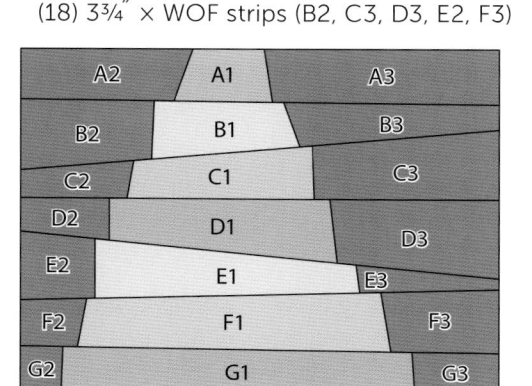

Block Diagram

Because the strips are long and thin, it can be difficult to keep the low volume fabrics from bunching on the foundation paper while pinning and piecing. To minimize this, try starching the low volume fabric strips before pinning them to the foundation. This will add a little stiffness and stability while you stitch the end pieces which were cut from the background fabric.

## ASSEMBLING THE BLOCK

Assemble 24 blocks, using the sequencing indicated on the pattern pieces.

## ASSEMBLING THE QUILT TOP

Construction Diagram

1. Referencing the Construction Diagram, arrange the blocks into four columns. Column 1 and Column 3 are identical, as are Columns 2 and 4.

2. Sew the blocks into columns.

3. Press the seams of odd-numbered columns up and even-numbered columns down.

4. Sew the columns together. All seams should nest nicely. Press.

## FINISHING

1. Layer the quilt top with the batting and backing fabric, then baste and quilt as desired.

2. Attach the binding using your favorite method.

## The Exercises

Look to nature for your inspiration for this exercise. Shapes in nature tend to be complicated; there are curves, minute details and intricate patterns that can be overwhelming. Train your eye to look at an object and focus only on the most significant shapes or just one simple detail. If you are looking at a flower, consider just the general shape of a petal instead of the layering and overlapping. Rather than looking at the rounded shape of a leaf, focus on the angular veins only. Look for a detail or an overarching shape that will be successful for this exercise.

Sometimes it helps to base your drawing on what you remember of that object. This automatically removes many details and minutia that may distract you, and releases you from the expectation that your design will be realistic, which isn't the goal for this exercise.

Instead of looking to a traditional star block, I used the idea of a star as my inspiration for Luminous. I made a simple four-square and decided that the points of the stars would match at the seam lines. Beyond that, the block is improvisationally styled with random widths and lengths for each arm. This is a more complicated block to draw than the patterns we have explored so far. Before you draft one as complex, be sure you have developed a solid understanding of paper-pieced block construction.

## Luminous

**FINISHED BLOCK SIZE**
10˝ square

**FINISHED QUILT SIZE**
50˝ × 60˝

**NUMBER OF BLOCKS**
30 (including partial blocks)

## Setting

It was only when I began adding color to the improvised block that I discovered an overlapping pattern that could be created by piecing each arm with a different solid. It's the kind of discovery that you will sometimes make only while improvising. So, I experimented with different color placements in my computer software program. Because the color combinations alone were so exciting, I really didn't feel the need to introduce more movement through anything other than a traditional grid setting.

## Fabric and Quilting

Each block is pieced with solids in varying shades of yellow, red, and orange. Each point is pieced with one solid. The order of the colors is random in each, so that no two blocks are the same.

While arranging them, I twisted and turned them to create an improvisational feel. Each star looks a bit different from the next, yet the repetition makes your eye move around the composition and follow the similar shapes from block to block. By placing partial blocks around the perimeter, the design appears to extend beyond the quilt—just like a starry sky!

## Materials List

Orange Solids in 5 different shades ranging from yellow to red tones: 1 yard each

Background Fabric: 4 yards

Backing Fabric: 3¾ yards

Binding Fabric: ½ yard

Batting: 56″ × 66″

## PREPARATION

Print 30 copies of each of the Luminous Pattern Pieces A-D. Each block contains 4 sections per block (see pages 136-139).

## CUTTING

From the assorted orange fabrics, cut:
  (120) 2½″ × 4½″ strips (A2, B2, C2, D2)
  (90) 2½″ × 5½″ strips (A3, B3, C3)
  (30) 2½″ × 7″ strips (D3)
  (120) 2½″ × 6″ strips (A5, B5, C5, D5)

> If you wish to make each arm of the star the same color, as I did, you must pair Sections A2 and B5, B2 and C5, C2 and D5, and A5 and D2 with the same colors when cutting and piecing. It's helpful to stack your sections in the order in which they will be assembled so that you can visualize this and keep them in the correct sequence.

From the grey background fabric, cut:
  (30) 4″ × 5″ rectangles (A1)
  (30) 3½″ × 6″ rectangles (A4)
  (30) 4″ × 5″ rectangles (B1)
  (30) 4½″ × 6″ rectangles (B4)
  (30) 4″ × 5″ rectangles (C1)
  (30) 4½″ × 6″ rectangles (C4)
  (30) 4″ × 6″ rectangles (D1)
  (30) 4½″ × 6″ rectangles (D4)

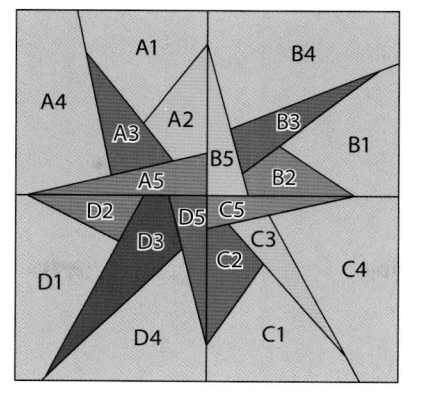

Block Diagram

## ASSEMBLING THE BLOCK

Assemble the sections for 30 blocks. Keep them grouped as complete blocks in order to keep the colors straight, but do not sew Sections A–D together yet.

## ASSEMBLING THE QUILT TOP

Contruction Diagram

1. Referencing the Construction Diagram, arrange the blocks. The inner portion of the quilt is a simple 4 x 5 grid with completed blocks (all 4 quadrants). Each block was randomly turned to the side or upside down.

2. The border is composed of half-blocks (2 quadrants). One of the Sections from the last block is placed in the four corners.

3. Sew the block quardants into rows.

4. Press the seams of odd-numbered rows to the right and even-numbered rows to the left.

5. Sew the rows together. All seams should nest nicely. Press.

## FINISHING

1. Layer the quilt top with the batting and backing fabric, then baste and quilt as desired.

2. Attach the binding using your favorite method.

# BONUS PATTERN

| B1 | A1 |
| B2 | A2 |
| B3 | A3 |
| B4 | A4 |
| B5 | A5 |
| B6 | A6 |
| B7 | A7 |
| B8 | A8 |
| B9 | A9 |
| B10 | A10 |
| B11 | A11 |

## Kite Tails

**FINISHED BLOCK SIZE**
12˝ × 18˝

**FINISHED QUILT SIZE**
60˝ × 72˝

**NUMBER OF BLOCKS**
20

*Kite Tails* is one of my earliest designs using the improv paper-piecing technique described in this book, and I am thrilled to share it here as a Bonus Pattern. As the name suggests, the design is based on the idea of kite tails.

I sewed it up as a scrappy quilt but it would be bold and daring in solids. The blocks are arranged in a grid, but the occasional block is inverted.

The piecing here inspires the quilting. I stitched crisscrossing lines of various spacing down the length of each column of kite tails.

As I mentioned earlier in this book, this is a great pattern to practice with. You may have already even made a few blocks to brush up on your paper-piecing technique. If you are eager to make some more, here is how to put this one together.

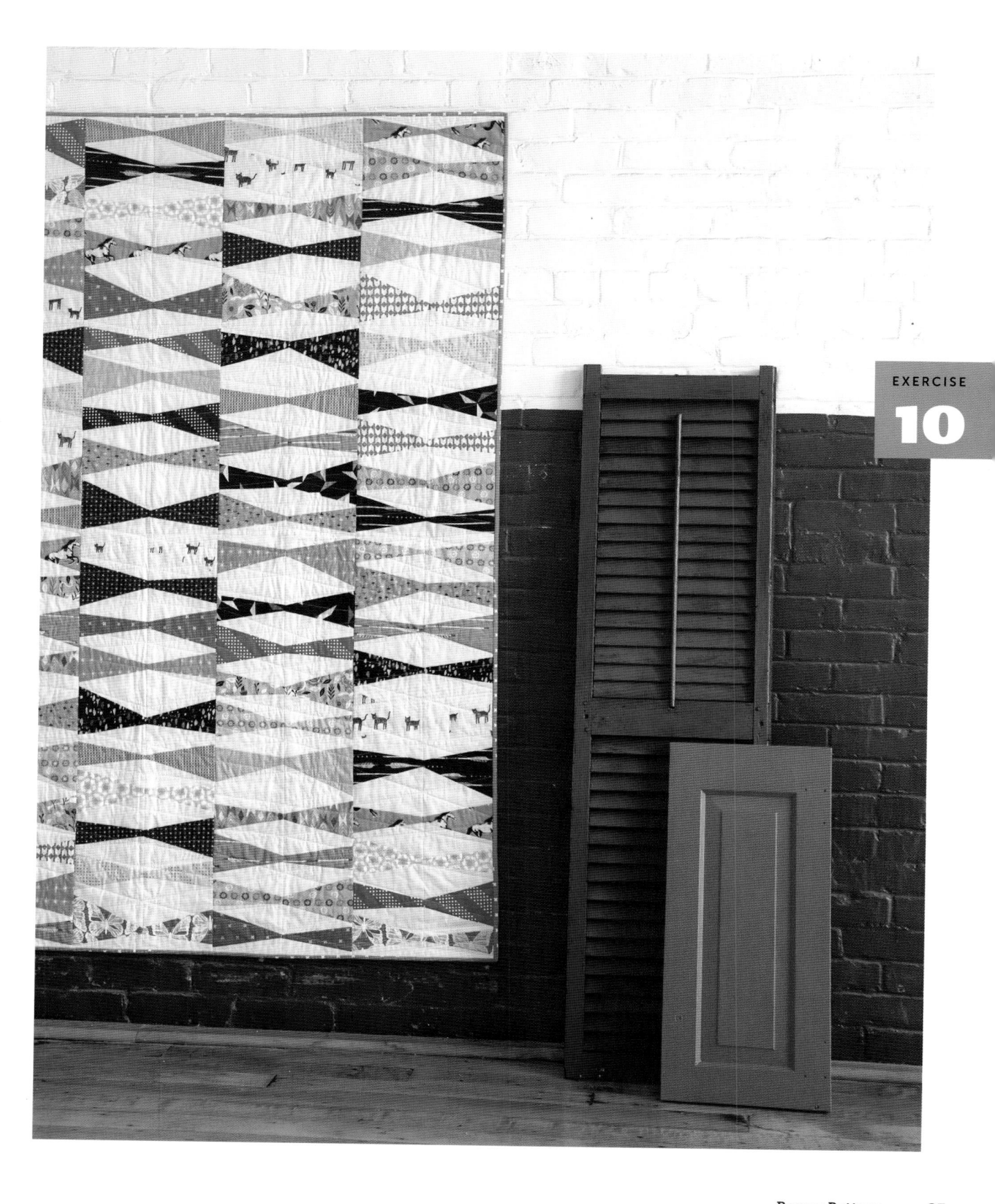

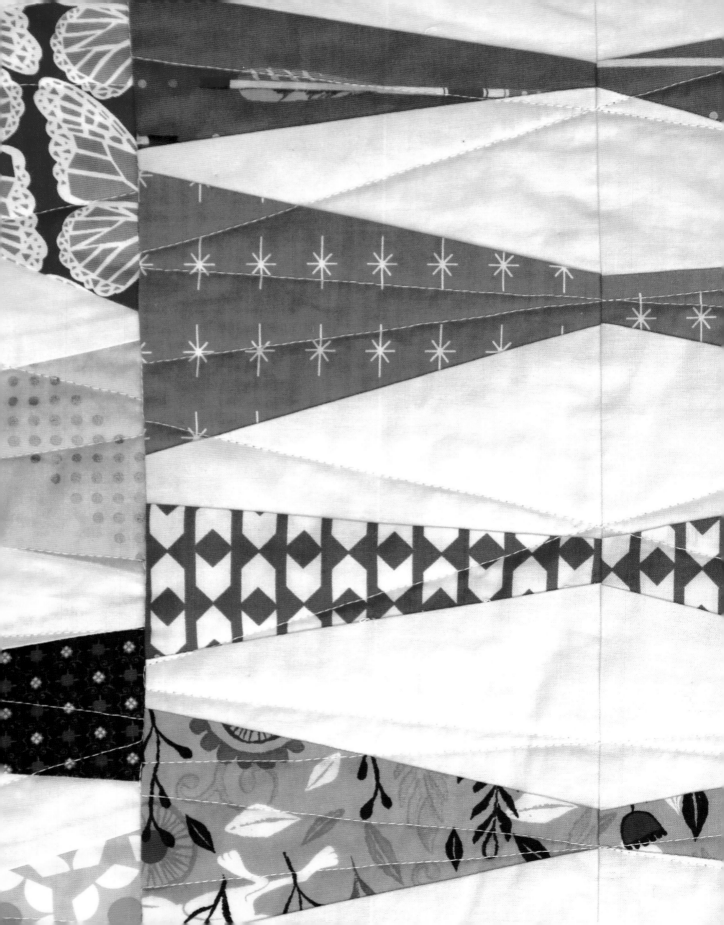

## Materials List

**Assorted Prints:** ¼ yard cuts of approximately 18–21 prints

**Background Fabric:** 4½ yards

**Backing Fabric:** 4¼ yards

**Binding Fabric:** ½ yard

**Batting:** 66˝ × 78˝

## PREPARATION

Print 20 copies of Template A and 20 copies of Template B (see pages 140 and 141).

## CUTTING

See the Advanced Paper-Piecing Tips (page 21-22) for cutting and piecing instructions for this block.

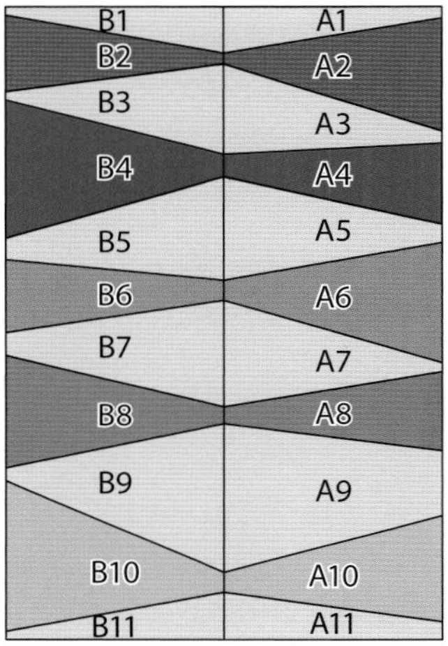

Block Diagram

## ASSEMBLING THE BLOCK

Assemble 20 blocks. If you are using directional prints, you may choose to invert some blocks prior to piecing in order to maintain directionality.

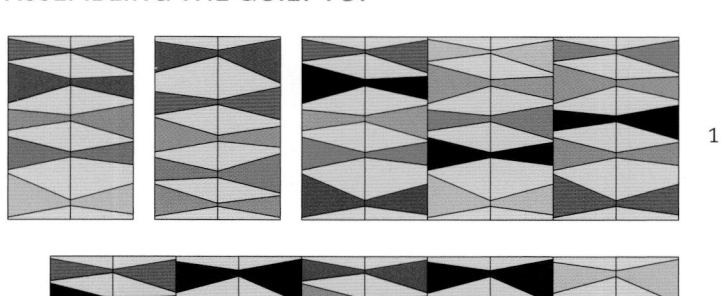

Inverted Blocks Diagram

## ASSEMBLING THE QUILT TOP

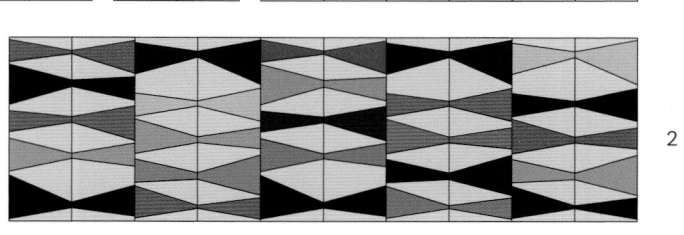

1

2

3

4

Construction Diagram

1. Arrange the blocks, consulting the Construction Diagram and Inverted Blocks Diagram (the arrows indicate inverted blocks).

2. Sew the blocks into rows.

3. Press the seams of odd-numbered rows to the right and even-numbered rows to the left.

4. Sew the rows together. All seams should nest nicely. Press.

## FINISHING

1. Layer the quilt top with the batting and backing fabric, then baste and quilt as desired.

2. Attach the binding using your favorite method.

*exploring* **different settings**

The success of an improvisationally designed paper-pieced block often lies in the layout. Once I create a block design, I start playing with different possibilities before I sew. Not every improvisationally drawn block will be successful, so I like to arrive at a setting idea before making a quilt top's worth of blocks only to regret it later.

You can use quilt design software, online mosaic makers, or apps for your phone. Search for key terms like "mosaic maker," "collage," and "photo editing" to find the most current applications available. You can even go "old school" and color your block on paper, photocopy it in multiples on a smaller scale, cut them out, and arrange them like puzzle pieces, taking pictures of each arrangement as you go.

Usually, my first step is to fill the quilt with blocks just as they were designed—a traditional quilt grid. Sometimes it works, like it did with my *Black Magic* quilt (see page 26). If it still doesn't seem quite right, you might then rotate some of the blocks and turn others upside down so that the repetition of the block isn't as immediately apparent and the shapes reinforce the improvisational feel.

But more often with these improv-drafted blocks, I find the traditional setting doesn't serve the block design best. Sometimes it is too busy due to the way the blocks interact along the seam lines. The blocks don't hold their own; they are not cohesive because they don't match up at their points to create surprising secondary patterns like their traditional relatives. They need more breathing room. Other times, the traditional grid is simply too stilted. Hopefully walking you through a few of my layout experiments will encourage you to do the same.

## Assembling the Block

My *Peacock Crossing* quilt is an example of a time when the traditional grid looked really stilted (Fig. 1). The slight irregularities of the piecing lines within the feather shape were not noticeable because my eye was hooked on the symmetrical, repeated shape.

Figure 1

Then, I rotated the blocks to bring the points together which created a secondary pinwheel design. It was closer to what I wanted, but there was too much negative space (Fig. 2).

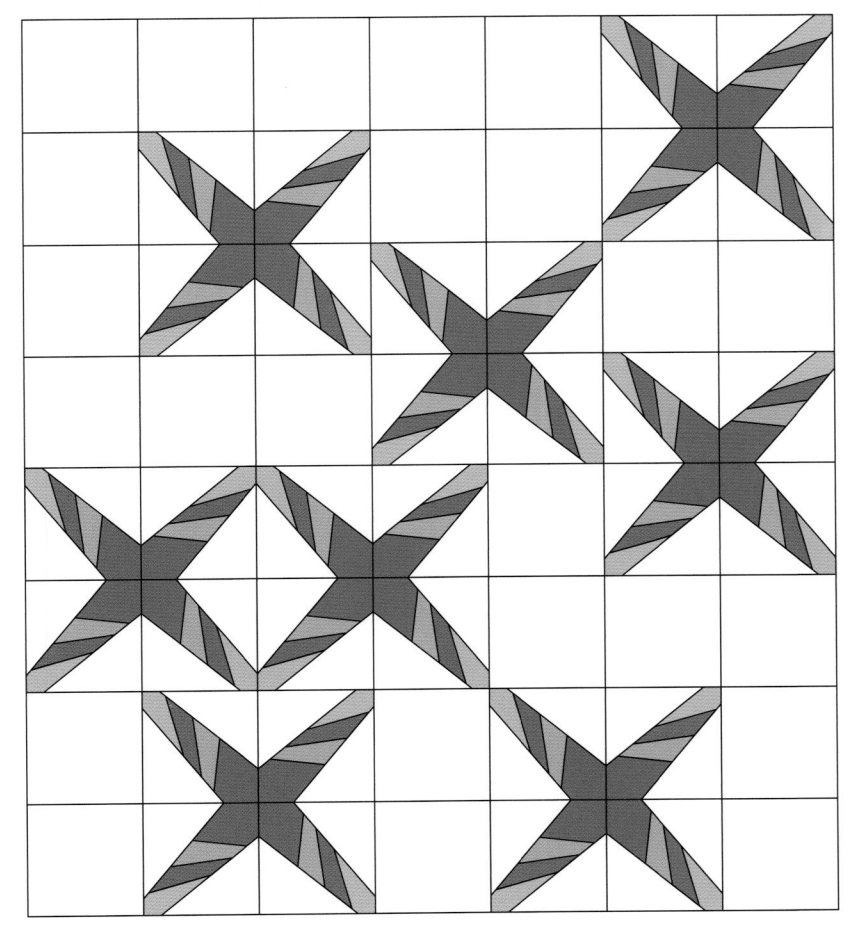

Figure 2

So I tried adding more blocks. This setting gave those shapes dominance, making them stand out and created a secondary pinwheel design, but the overall look still felt very traditional (Fig. 3). There was no visual tension. One more rotation led me to my final design (see page 50).

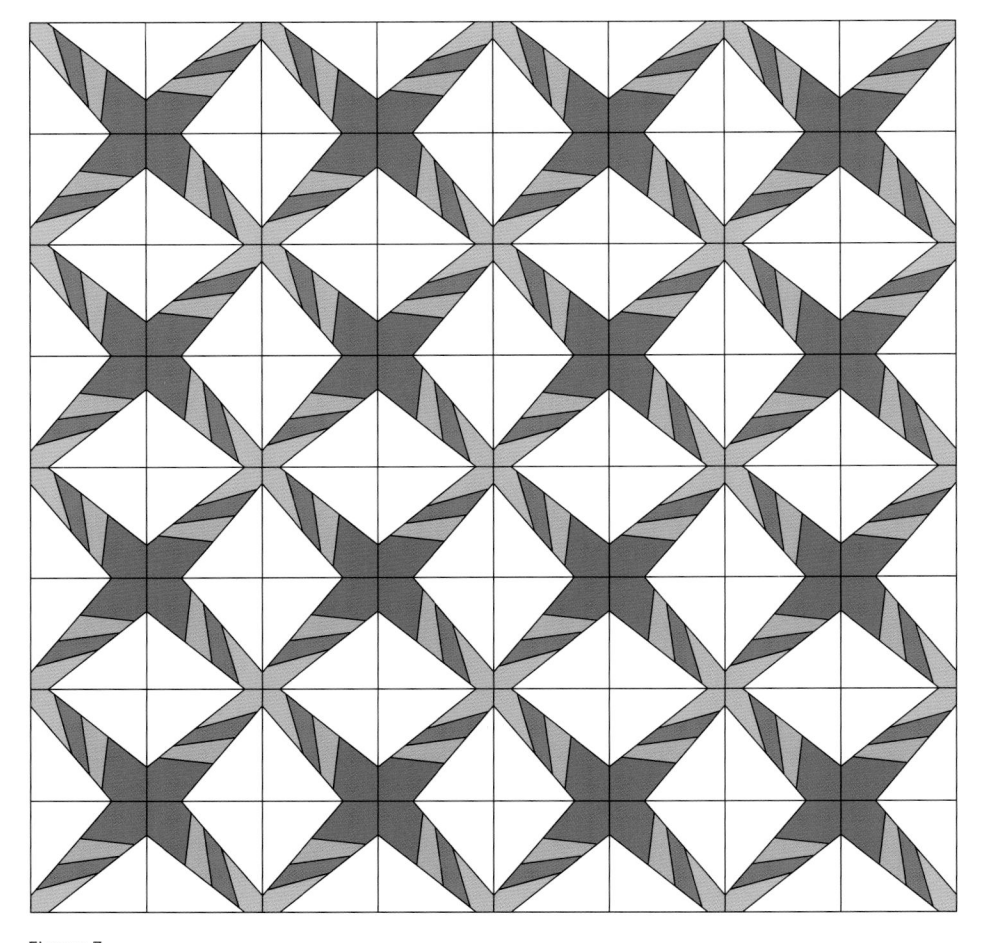

Figure 3

## When Less is More

Creating an alternate grid can really make a design work. Rather than organizing the blocks in columns and rows with many blocks, explore the effect created by increasing the negative space between the blocks. Shifting the grid to offset the columns is another favorite solution to play around with.

A prime example of 'less is more' is my reinterpretation of the Tallahassee block. Simply repeating it (Fig. 4) created some interesting negative space, but it was also rather busy and the individual blocks didn't hold together as a unit. When I added negative space and moved them out of their grid into a serpentine shape, the design was much stronger (Fig. 5).

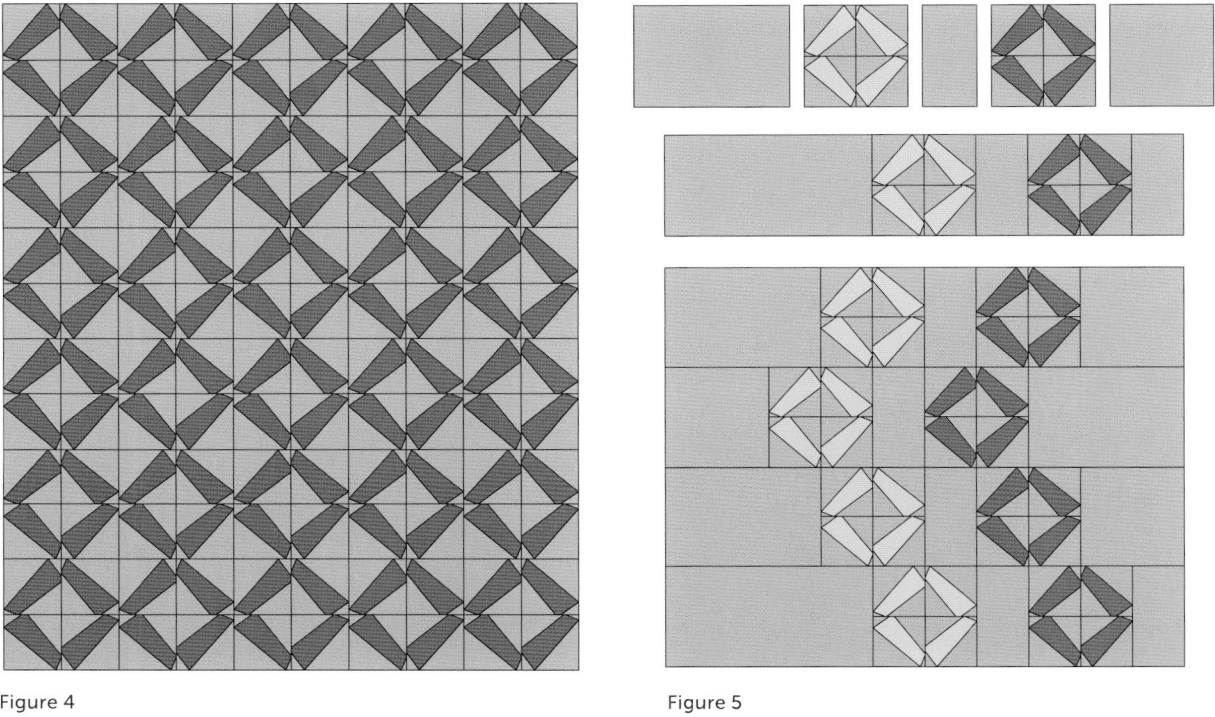

Figure 4

Figure 5

## Finding Secondary Patterns

For another example, let's look at my *Paper Trail* layout progression.
First, I lined up all the blocks in a traditional grid. This design really
didn't do anything for me (Fig. 6).

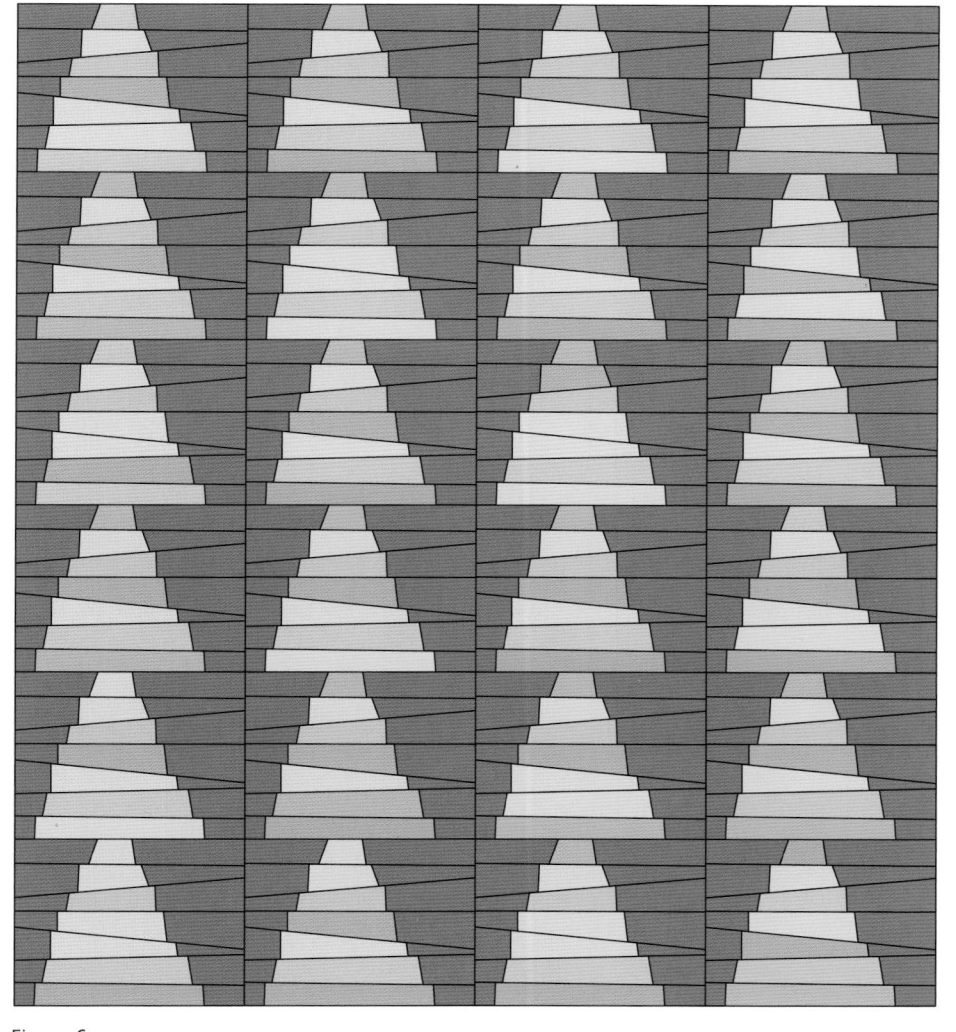

Figure 6

Next, I tried inverting every other block in the columns (Fig. 7). I started to get excited here. Because the blocks were improvisationally sketched and off-center, they didn't line up perfectly; this gave the design a feeling of motion and created a completely new shape with the joining of two blocks. But I felt it could be better still.

Figure 7

That's when I offset the rows (Fig. 8). The resulting grid just felt right.

Figure 8

# A Look in the Mirror

In addition to rotating and inverting some blocks and experimenting with alternate grid work, it is sometimes helpful to include the mirror image of the original block. When using the traditional Hourglass block design and adapting it for my *Sixty Seconds* quilt (Fig. 9), I realized that all of my lines were slanting in the same direction. By including the mirror image of the block, I added more variety and variation while still using only my original improv sketch.

Figure 9

# Finding Perspective

If you are using a design wall or the floor, step back when you arrive at a composition that you think you like. You will gain perspective this way rather than getting bogged down in details that aren't visible at a distance. If the design is on your monitor, get off your chair and stand across the room from the screen. If it is on paper, tack it to the wall and step back.

Take a picture with your phone and look at a thumbnail-size view. This serves the same purpose.

Next, tack that paper upside down or rotate the image on your screen. A good composition should still be strong even when inverted.

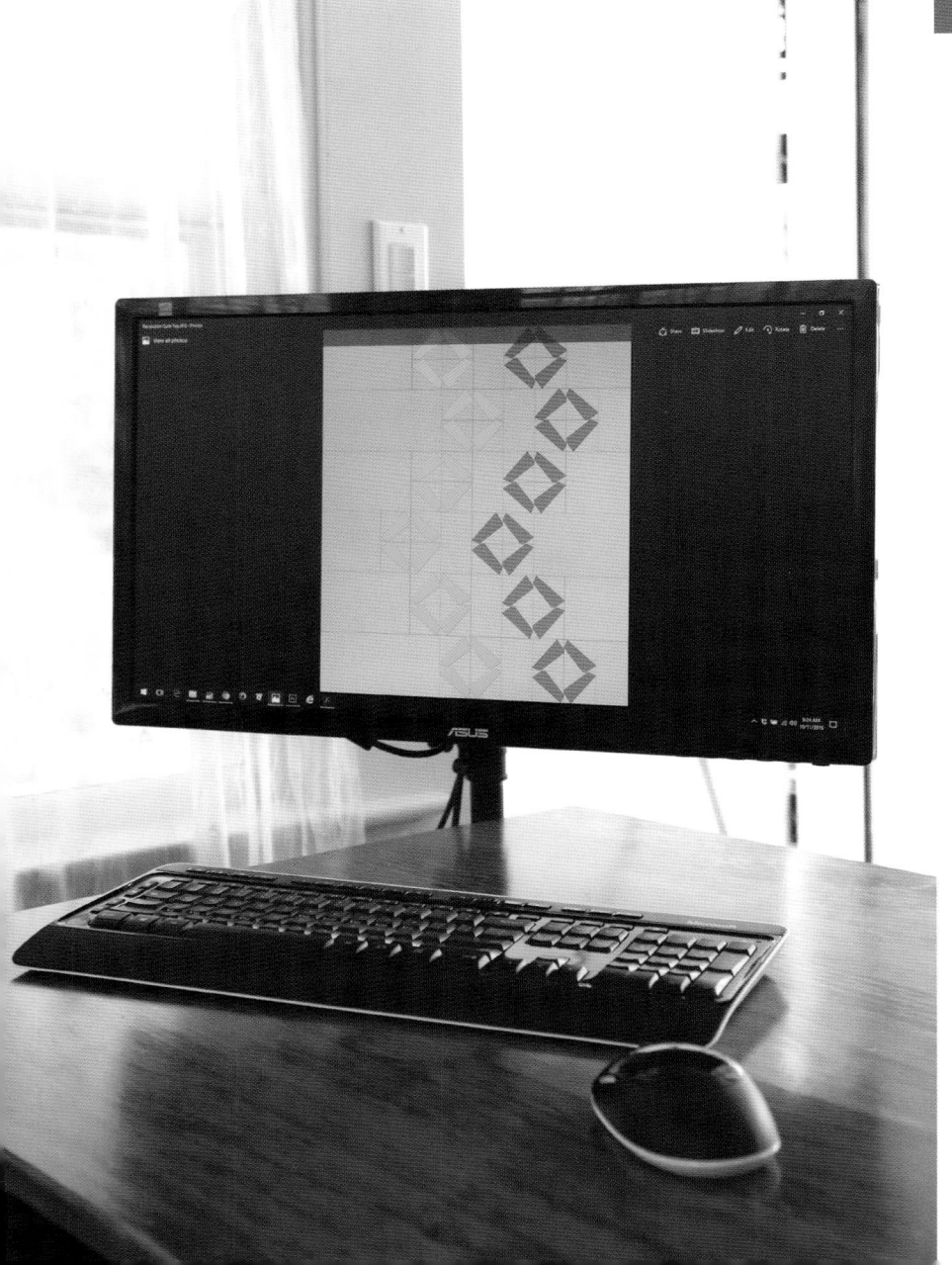

## experimenting with gridwork

- *Rotate your block to the side.*

- *Turn your block upside down.*

- *Use both your original block and the mirror image of that block.*

- *Create negative space.*

- *Go off the grid.*

- *Stagger blocks from row to row.*

- *Try two nearly identical blocks as a pair, or try two in different sizes.*

- *Look for a shape with dominance in the block design. If it is not there, create dominance through the setting.*

# faBRIC
## selecTions

## Solids, Prints or Scrappy

Quilt design is multilayered. In addition to the roles played by block design and gridwork, fabric selection is key. Fabric choices can really alter the overall look of the quilt.

Using scrappy prints contributes to the improvisational feel in many ways. Allow yourself to have fun piecing with reckless abandon, using what you have, and seeing what unexpected patterns might emerge due to your fabric choices. This approach definitely meshes with the improv process.

However, scrappy fabric placement also distracts the eye from the shapes created by improv sketching and then piecing. I prefer using solids or tone-on-tone prints for the majority of my designs because they allow the unique shapes in the piecing to shine through. It also makes their repetition more obvious.

Another possibility is repeating the same colors in each section of a block but using different prints. You'll still achieve that great scrappy look but you are also still likely to see repetition of shape.

The best way to find out what works for you and what does not, is to make a test block or two. Try a few possibilities...and then repeat!

*Fabric choices can really alter the overall look of the quilt.*

# finishing
# DESIGN
# touches

## Quilting and Binding Choices

As you know, quilting and binding are the final design choices in making any quilt.

The quilting choices contribute to the overall feel of the completed project. My personal preference for quilting modern quilts tends to be using a walking foot to create straight-line quilting. Sometimes I choose an improvisational-feeling pattern, such as an irregular grid. That choice obviously suits the improv flavor that we are hoping to achieve (see page 108).

I also love what I call a "regular/irregular grid." It's where I create a grid with evenly spaced lines either ¼" or ½" apart but placed randomly, not in a pattern (see page 109). I actually use a regular/irregular straight-line motif sometimes too. Other times, I usually find the best way to accentuate the irregularities of the piecing is through contrast. I layer strictly straight line or grid quilting on top of improv piecing because the juxtaposition is interesting.

Seam lines formed by paper piecing or just the block joins themselves can be distracting and impose an unwanted grid on your design. If you notice sharp vertical seam lines, try quilting straight lines in the opposite direction to negate them (see page 110 and 111). Finding a good match for your quilting can enhance your improv efforts.

> *The best way to accentuate the irregularities of the piecing is through contrast.*

Quilting an Irregular Grid

Quilting a Regular/Irregular Grid

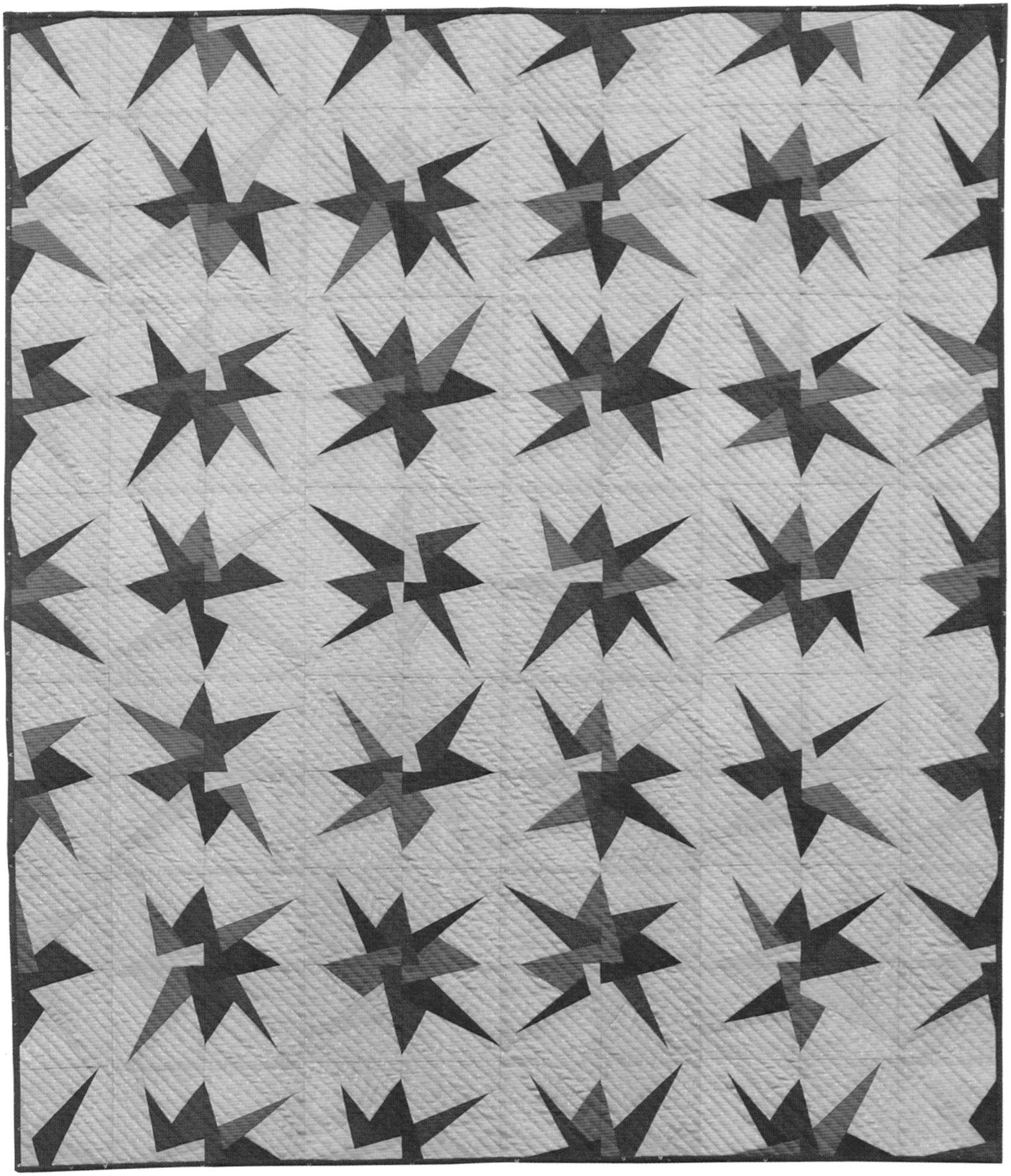

Straight-Line Quilting

Straight-Line Quilting

## Binding

Binding is an often-overlooked design element. A bold binding choice frames the composition like I used in *Revolution* (below). Choosing a binding in the same color as the background fabric or the pieced fabric closest to the edges makes the design appear to extend beyond the space. The composition isn't boxed in. If the quilt is made with a limited palette in order to focus on the shapes of the piecing, it could be fun to throw in a new color not yet introduced in the quilt to add a dash of the unexpected like in *Black Magic*.

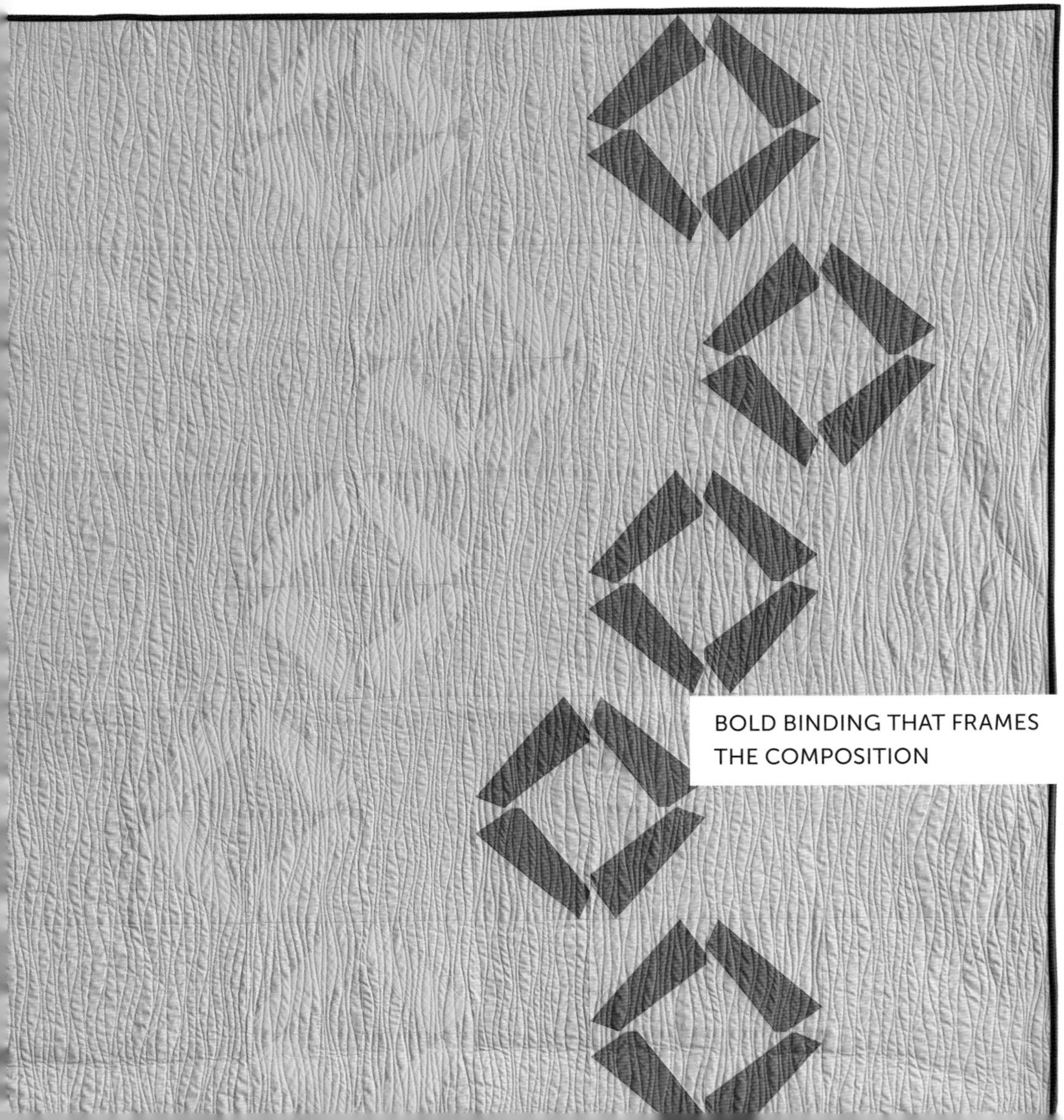

BOLD BINDING THAT FRAMES THE COMPOSITION

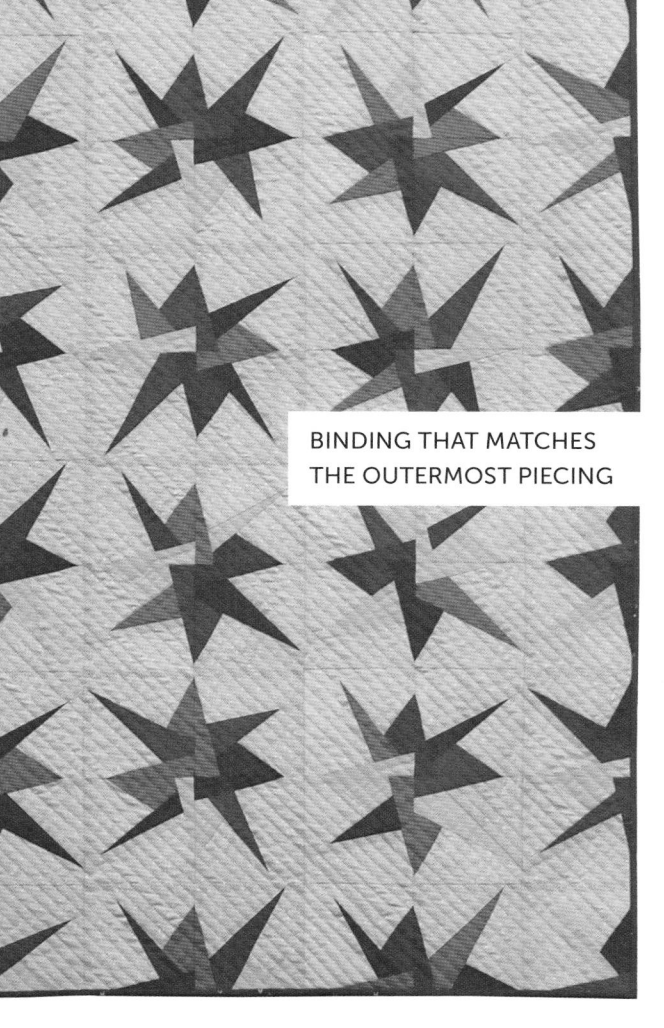

BINDING THAT MATCHES
THE OUTERMOST PIECING

BINDING THAT MATCHES THE BACKGROUND

BINDING THAT INTRODUCES
A NEW COLOR

# traditional block-based

## BASED

### design prompts

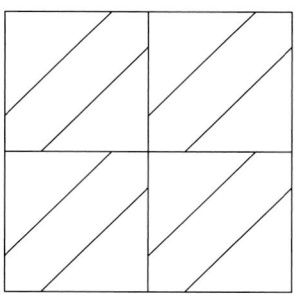

Album Block

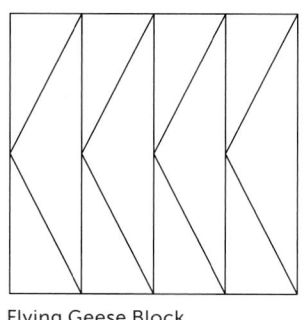

Flying Geese Block

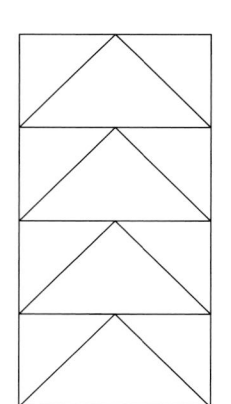

Flying Geese Block #2

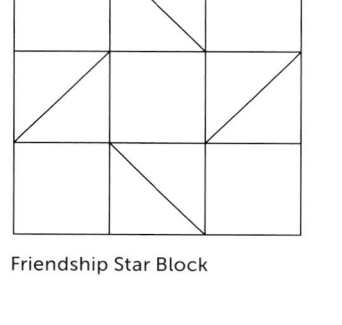

Friendship Star Block

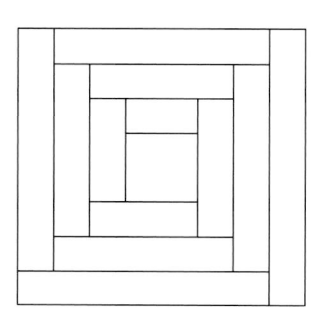

Log Cabin Block

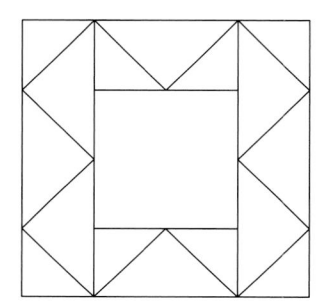

Mosaic Block

Rail Fence Block

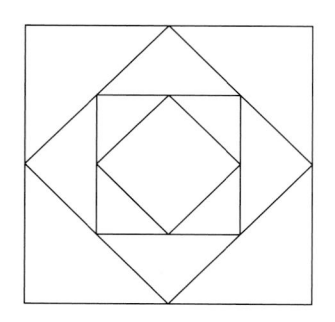

Square-in-a-Square Block

*Any one of these traditional blocks can be successfully adapted into an improvisationally designed paper-pieced block.*

# shape-
# BaSED
## *design prompts*

Square Design

Rectangle Design

*Start by drawing a symmetrical shape, then play with the lines. Vary the size and shape of your block. Or begin with an asymmetrical shape. Add borders and lines within it.*

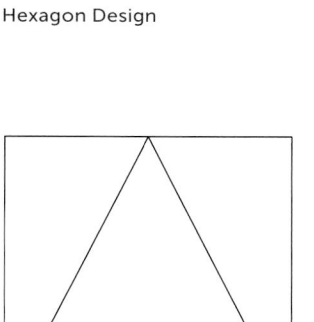

Hexagon Design

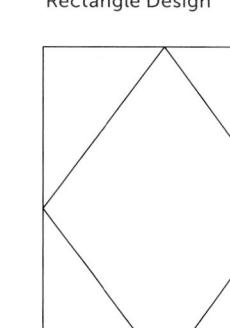

Symetrical Design

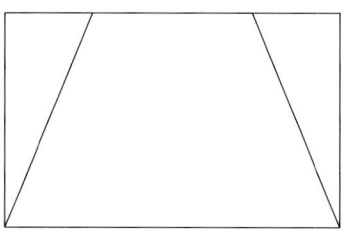

Trapezoid Design

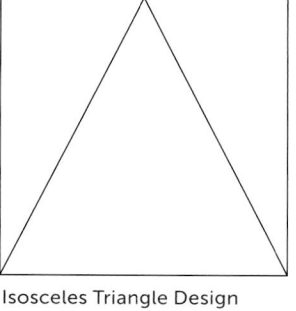

Isosceles Triangle Design

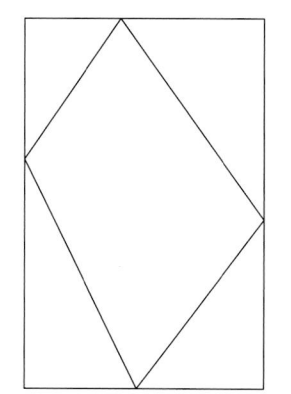

Asymmetrical Diamond Design

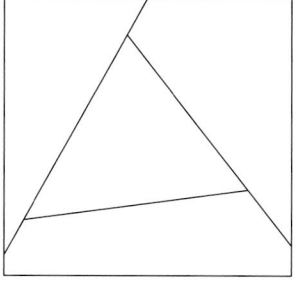

Asymmetrical Triangle Design

# object-BASED
## *design prompts*

Architecture • Fences • Street Signs
Flowers • Leaves • Toys • Tools • Furniture

Inspiration is all around you if you only look.

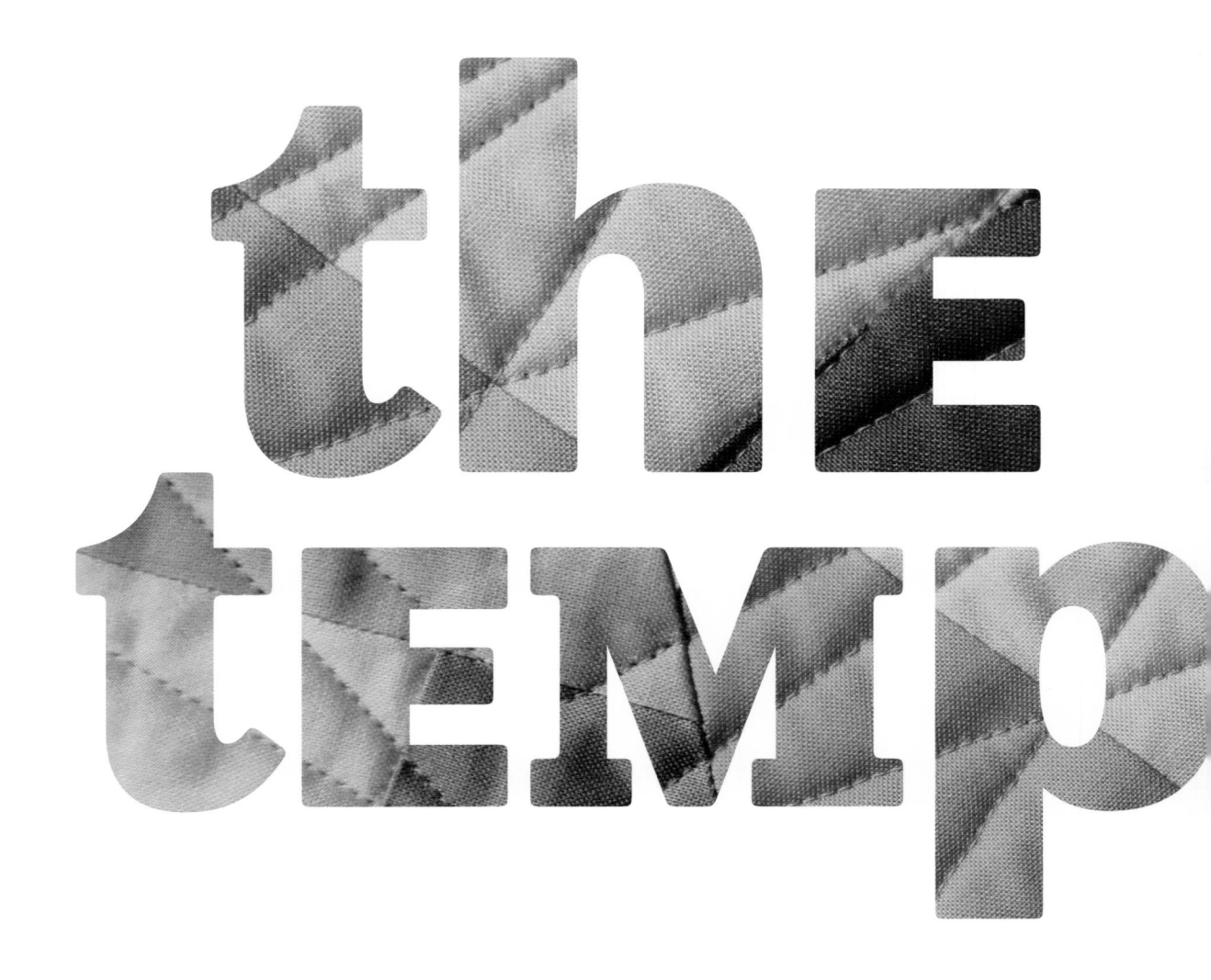

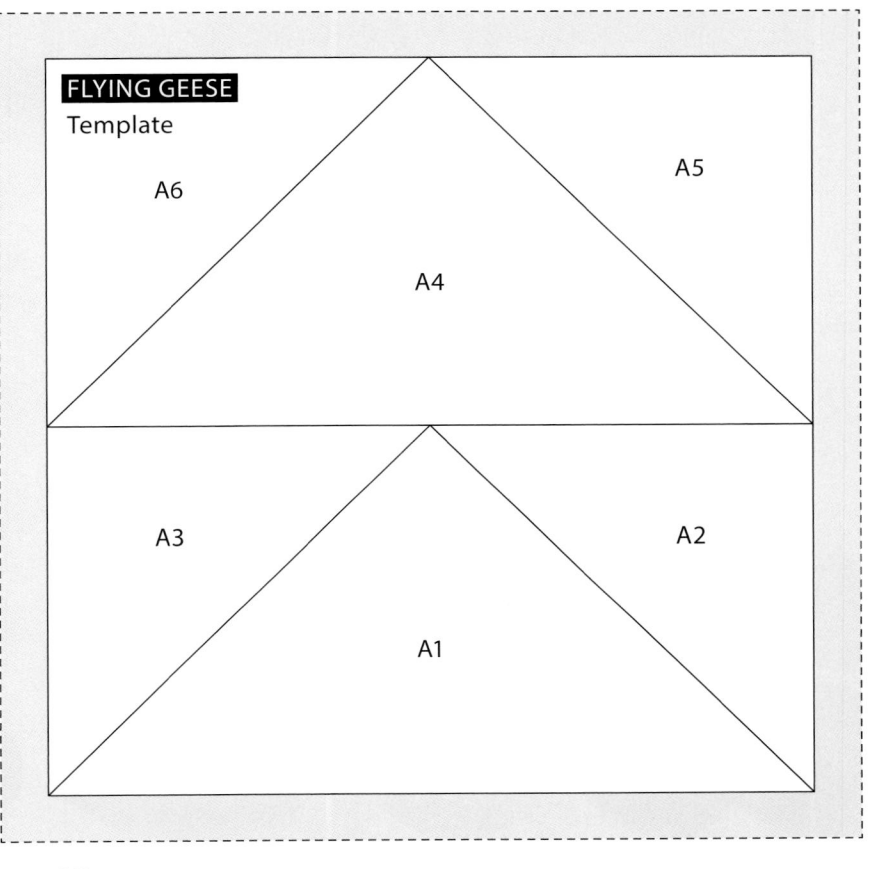

**FLYING GEESE**
Template

A6

A5

A4

A3

A2

A1

Actual Size

- - - cut line

—— stitch line

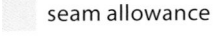 seam allowance

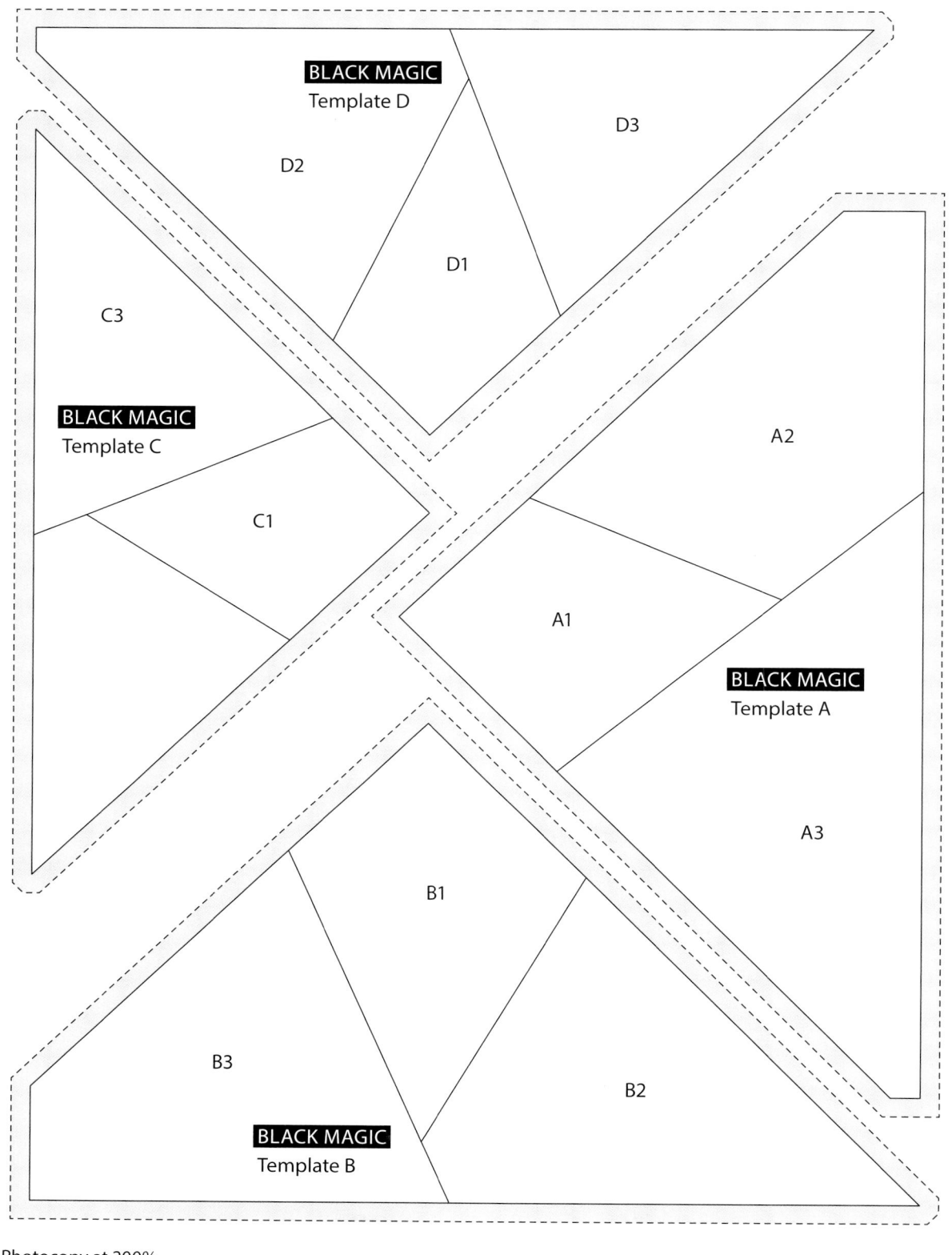

**BLACK MAGIC**
Template D

D2

D3

D1

C3

**BLACK MAGIC**
Template C

C1

A2

A1

**BLACK MAGIC**
Template A

A3

B1

B3

B2

**BLACK MAGIC**
Template B

Photocopy at 200%

- - - cut line

—— stitch line

seam allowance

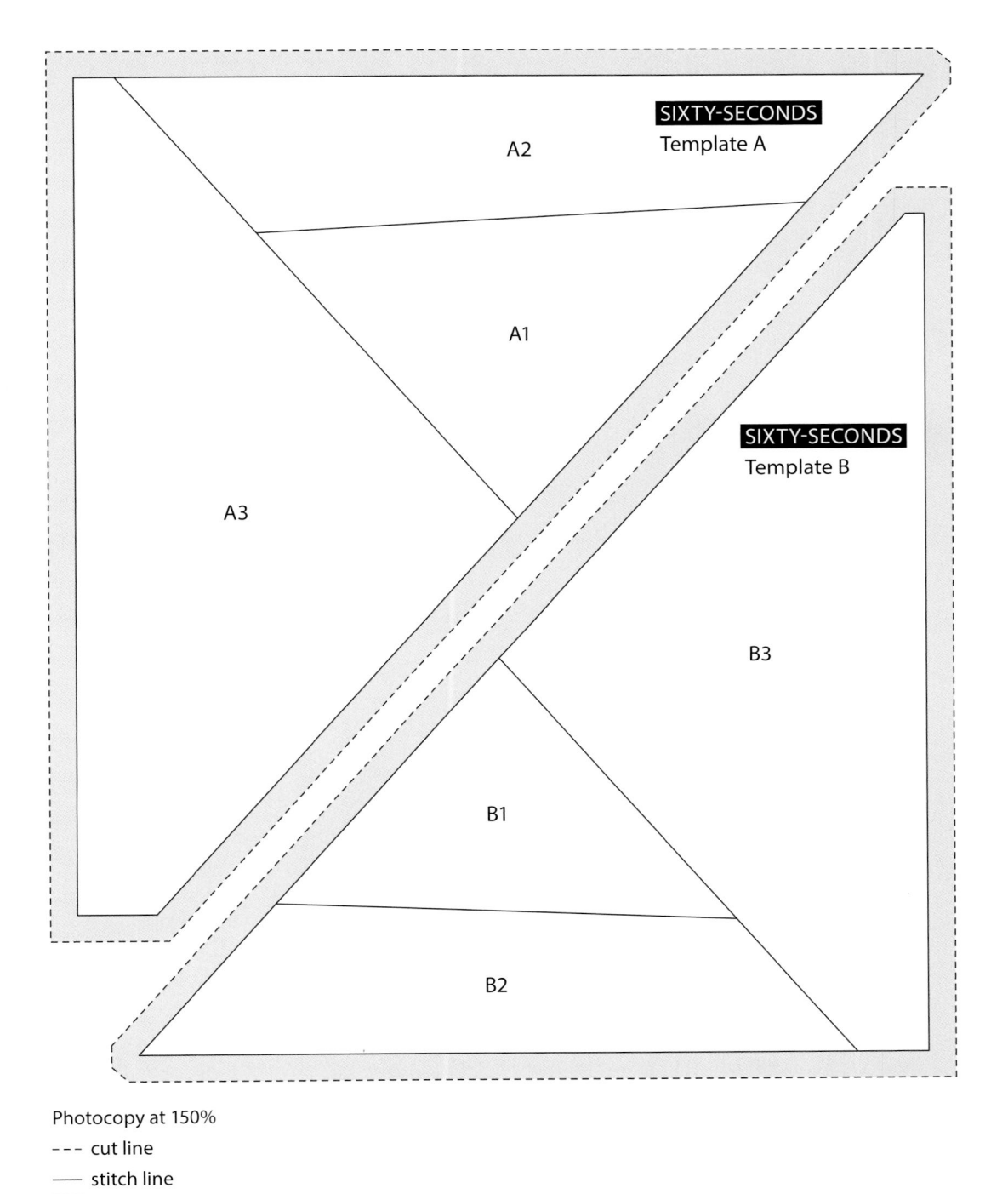

**SIXTY-SECONDS**
Template A

A2

A1

A3

**SIXTY-SECONDS**
Template B

B3

B1

B2

Photocopy at 150%

--- cut line
—— stitch line
seam allowance

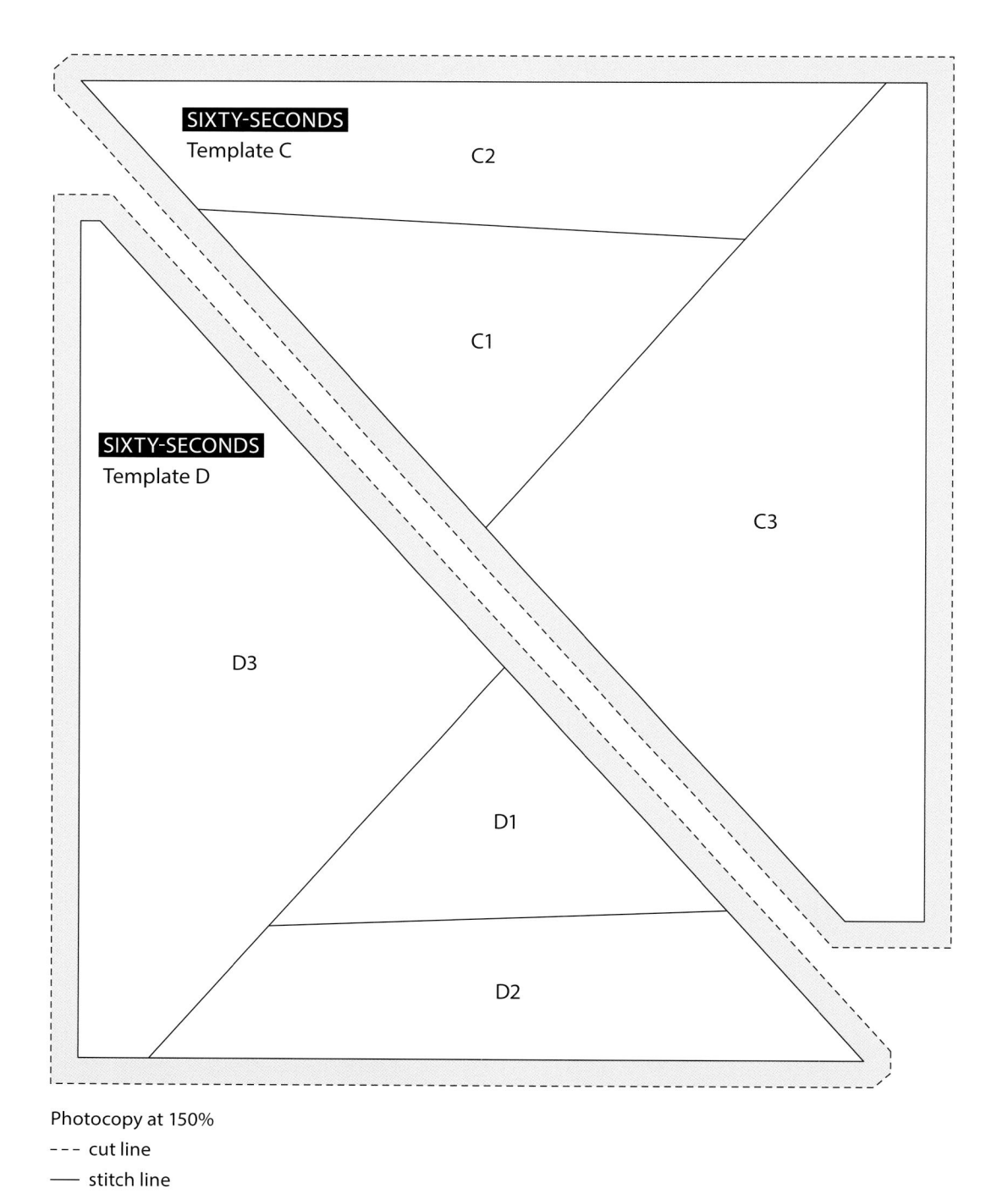

SIXTY-SECONDS
Template C

C2

C1

C3

SIXTY-SECONDS
Template D

D3

D1

D2

Photocopy at 150%

- - - cut line

—— stitch line

seam allowance

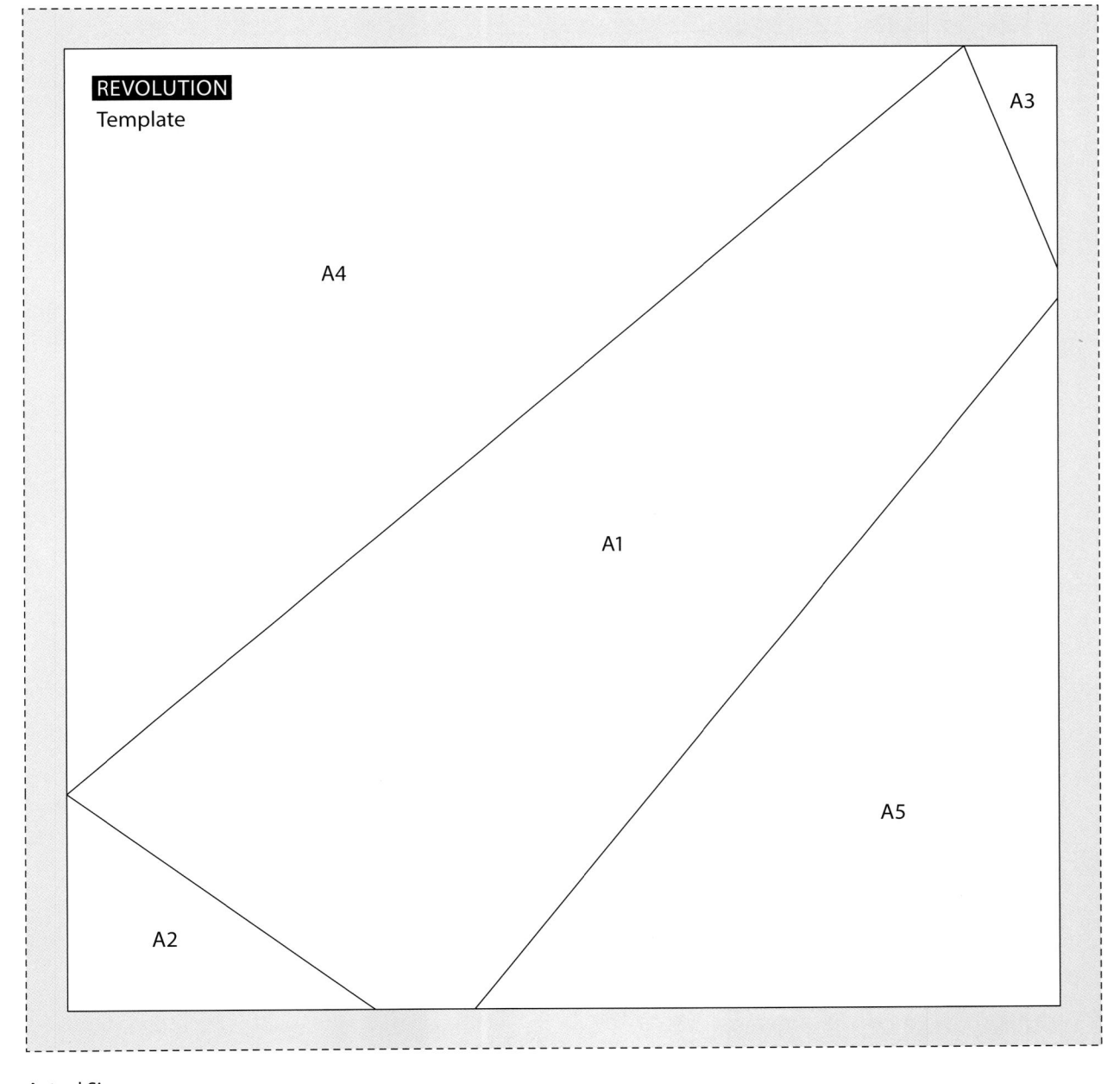

REVOLUTION
Template

A4

A3

A1

A2

A5

Actual Size

- - - cut line
—— stitch line
▢ seam allowance

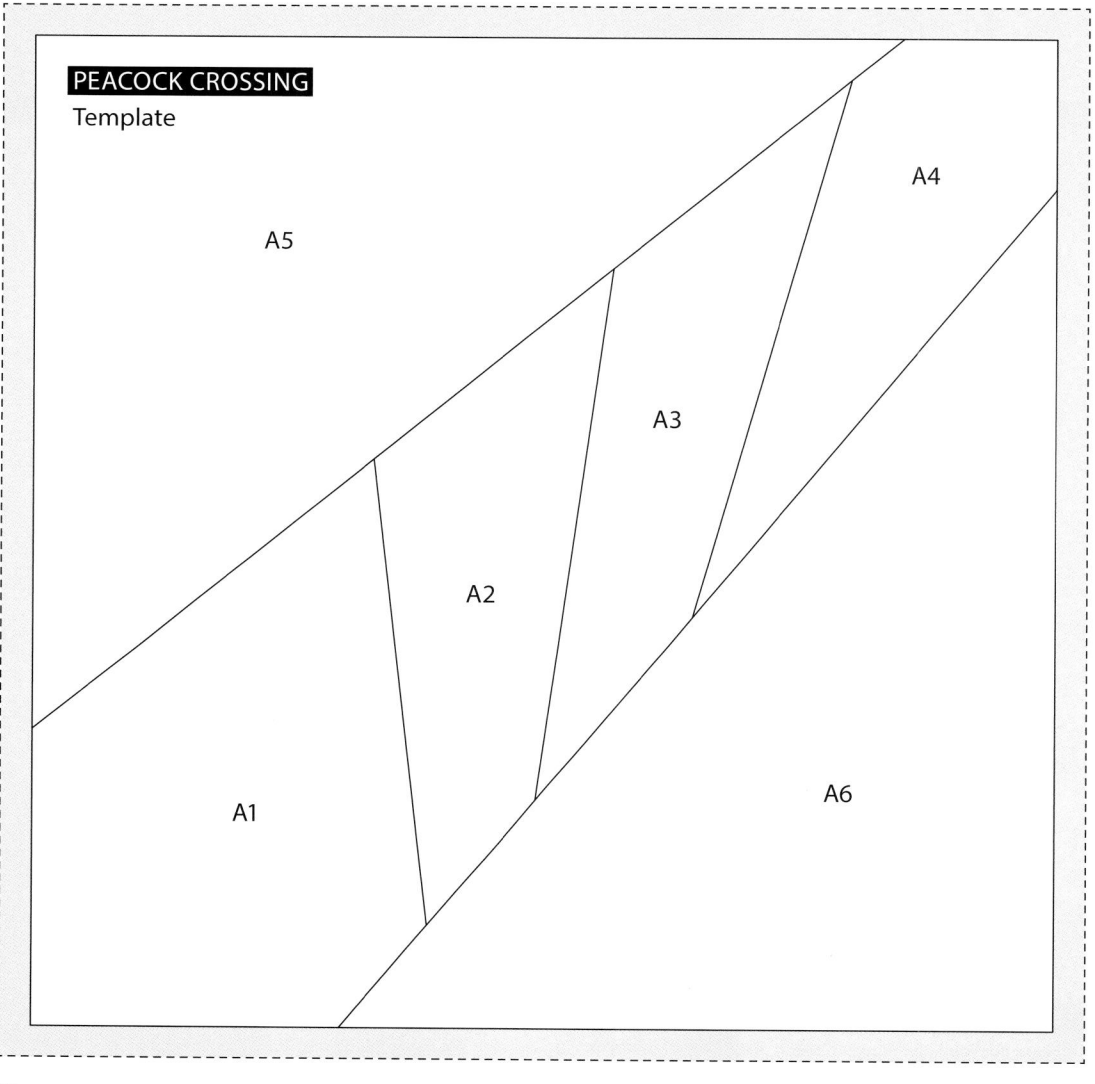

**PEACOCK CROSSING**
Template

A5

A4

A3

A2

A1

A6

Photocopy at 150%

- - - cut line

—— stitch line

▨ seam allowance

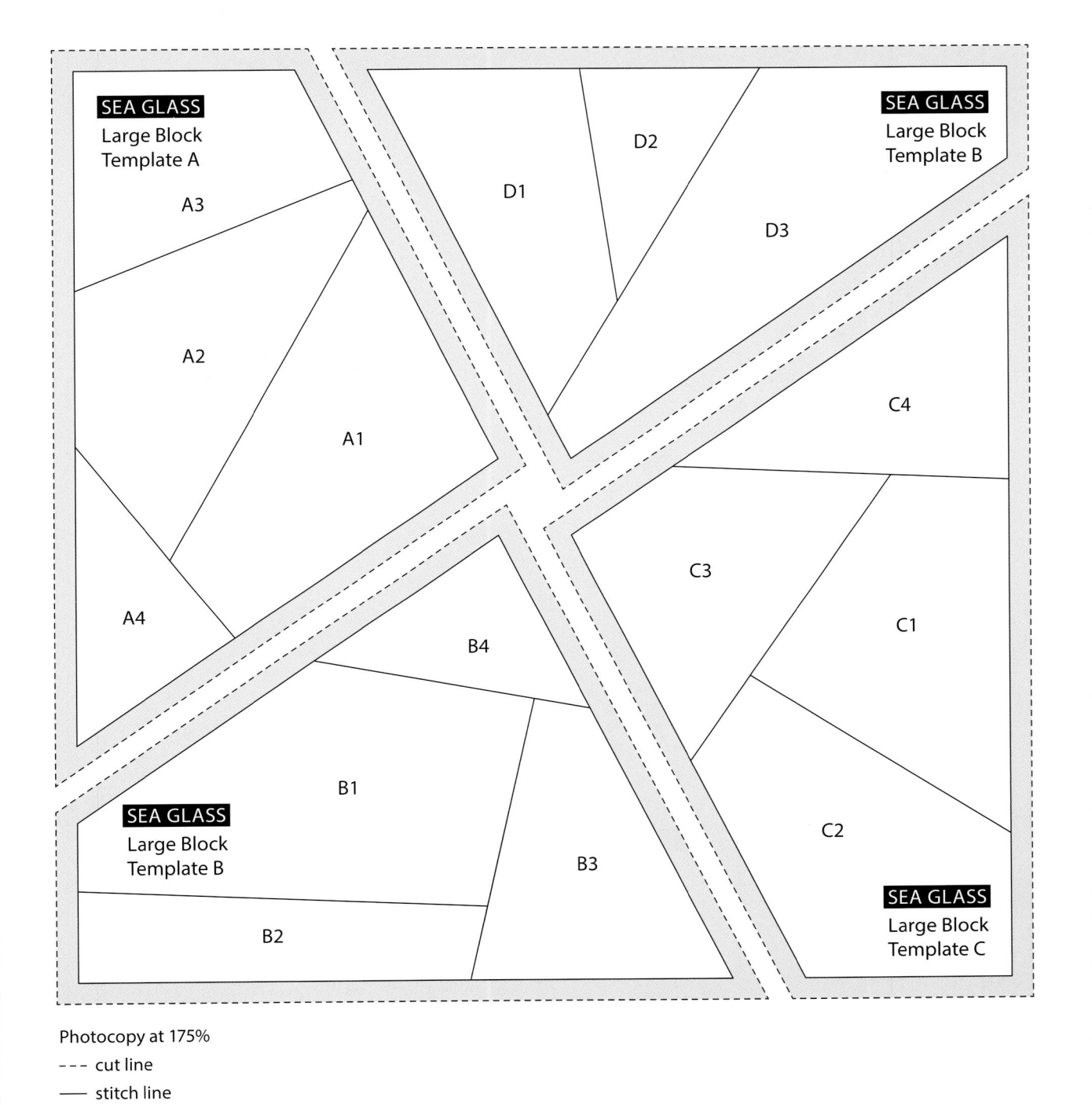

SEA GLASS
Large Block
Template A

A3

A2

A1

A4

SEA GLASS
Large Block
Template B

B1

B2

B4

B3

D1

D2

D3

SEA GLASS
Large Block
Template B

C4

C3

C1

C2

SEA GLASS
Large Block
Template C

Photocopy at 175%

- - - cut line

—— stitch line

    seam allowance

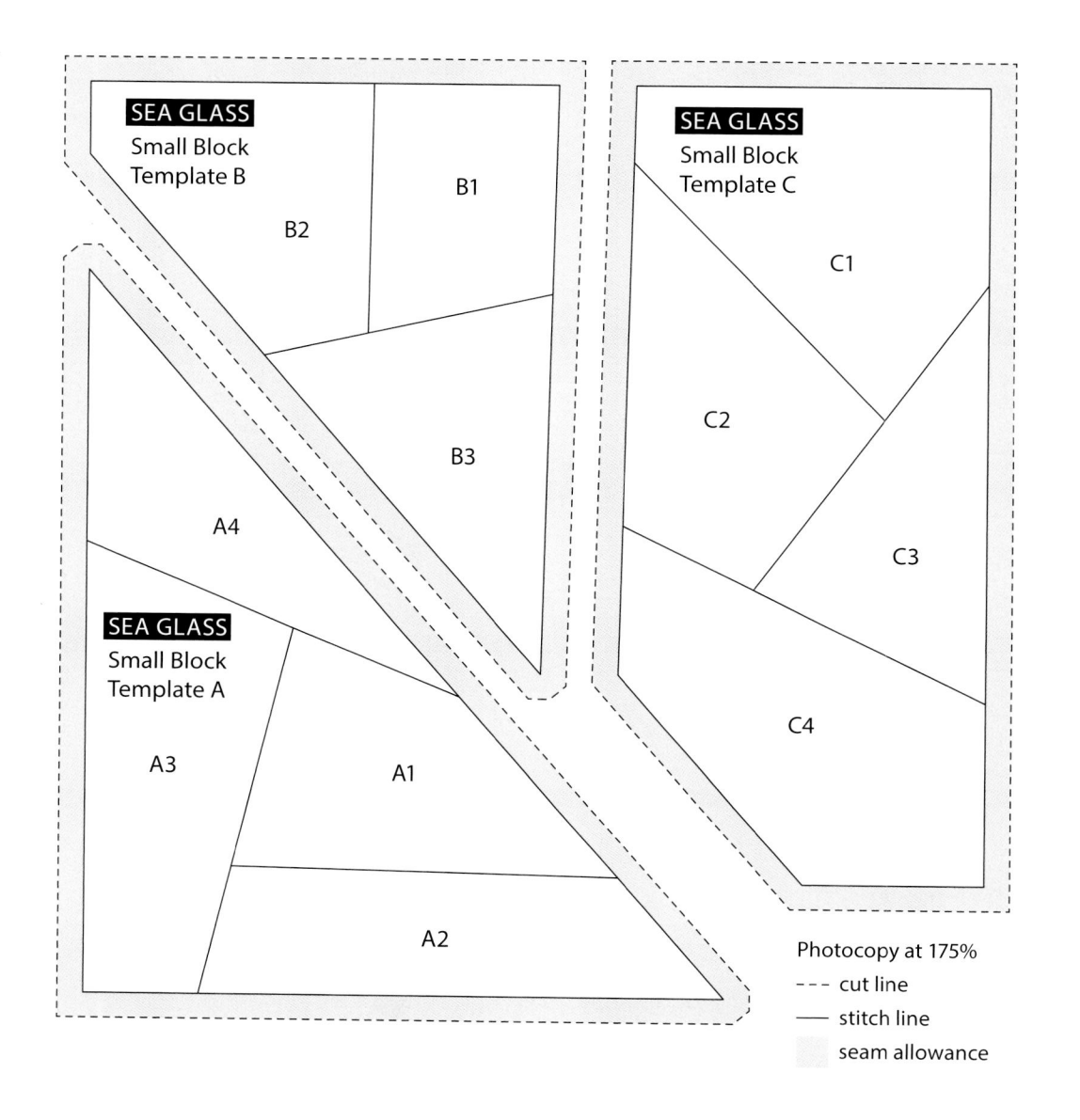

**SEA GLASS**
Small Block
Template B

B1

B2

B3

**SEA GLASS**
Small Block
Template A

A4

A3

A1

A2

**SEA GLASS**
Small Block
Template C

C1

C2

C3

C4

Photocopy at 175%
- - - cut line
——— stitch line
▨ seam allowance

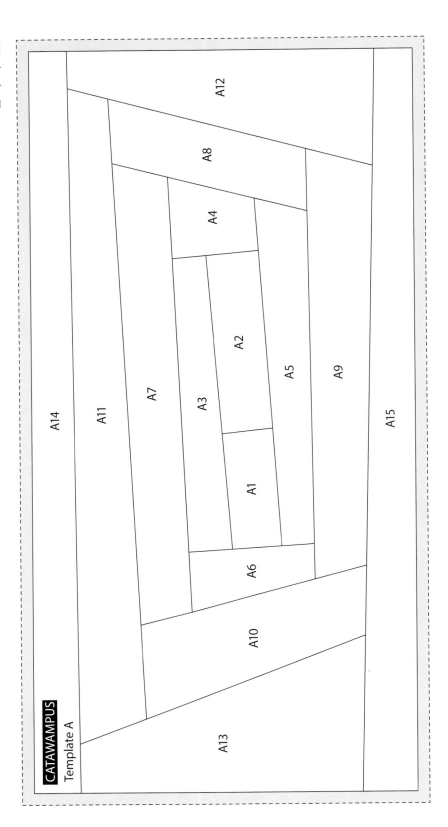

Photocopy at 200%
- - - cut line
—— stitch line
▨ seam allowance

CATAWAMPUS
Template A

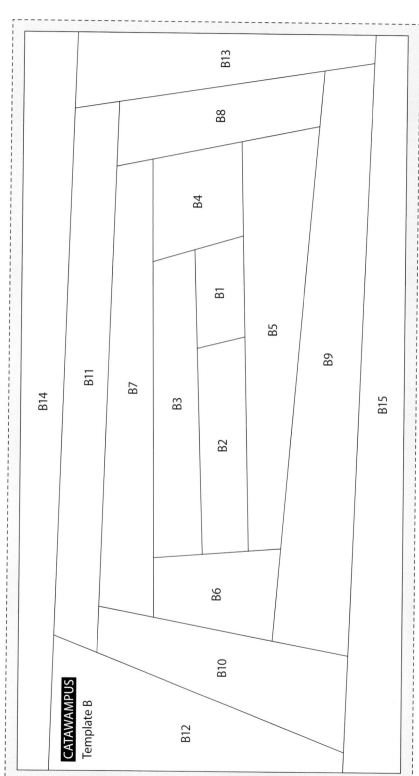

seam allowance
—— stitch line
--- cut line
Photocopy at 200%

**CATAWAMPUS**
Template B

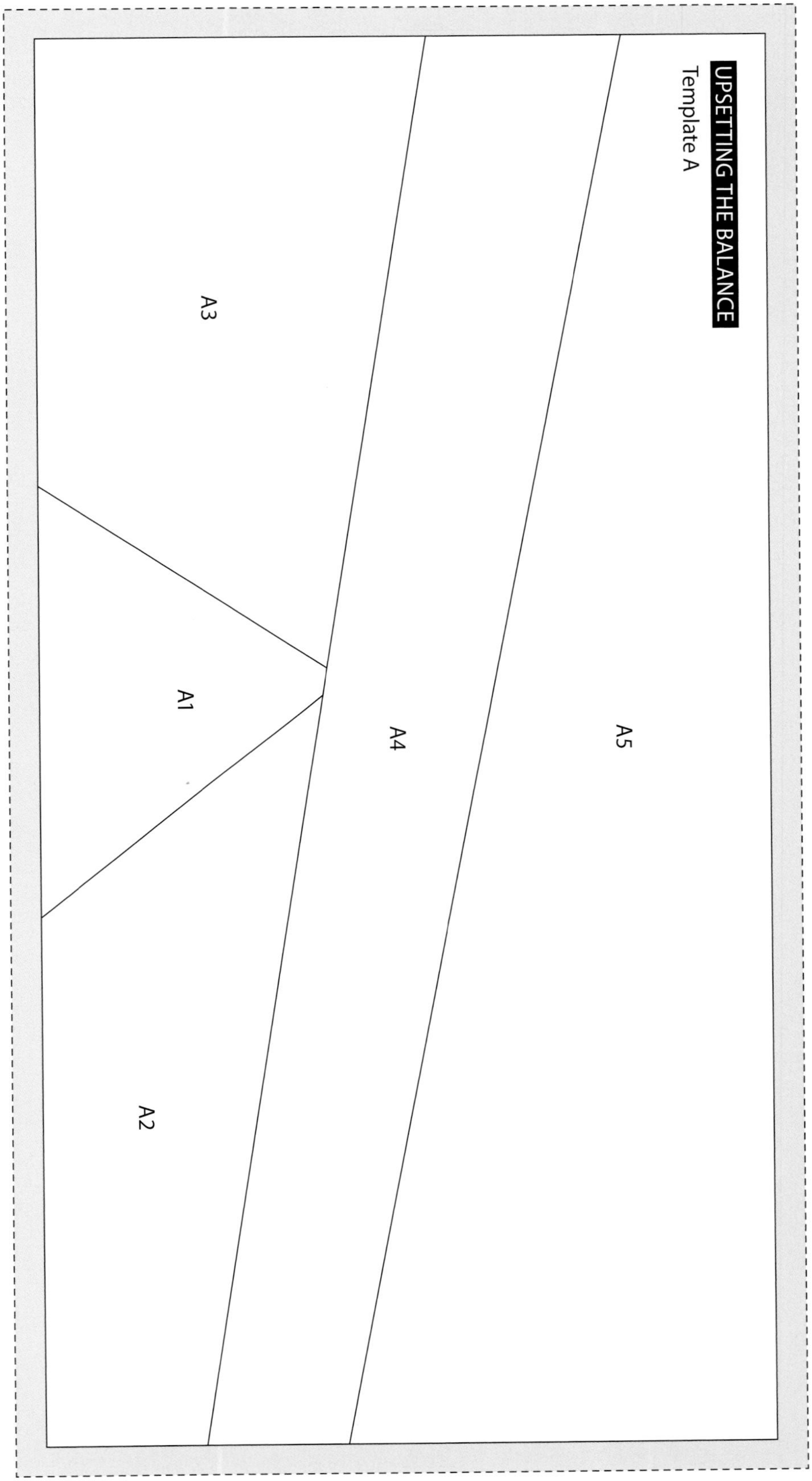

UPSETTING THE BALANCE

Template A

A3

A1

A4

A5

A2

Photocopy at 140%

--- cut line

— stitch line

seam allowance

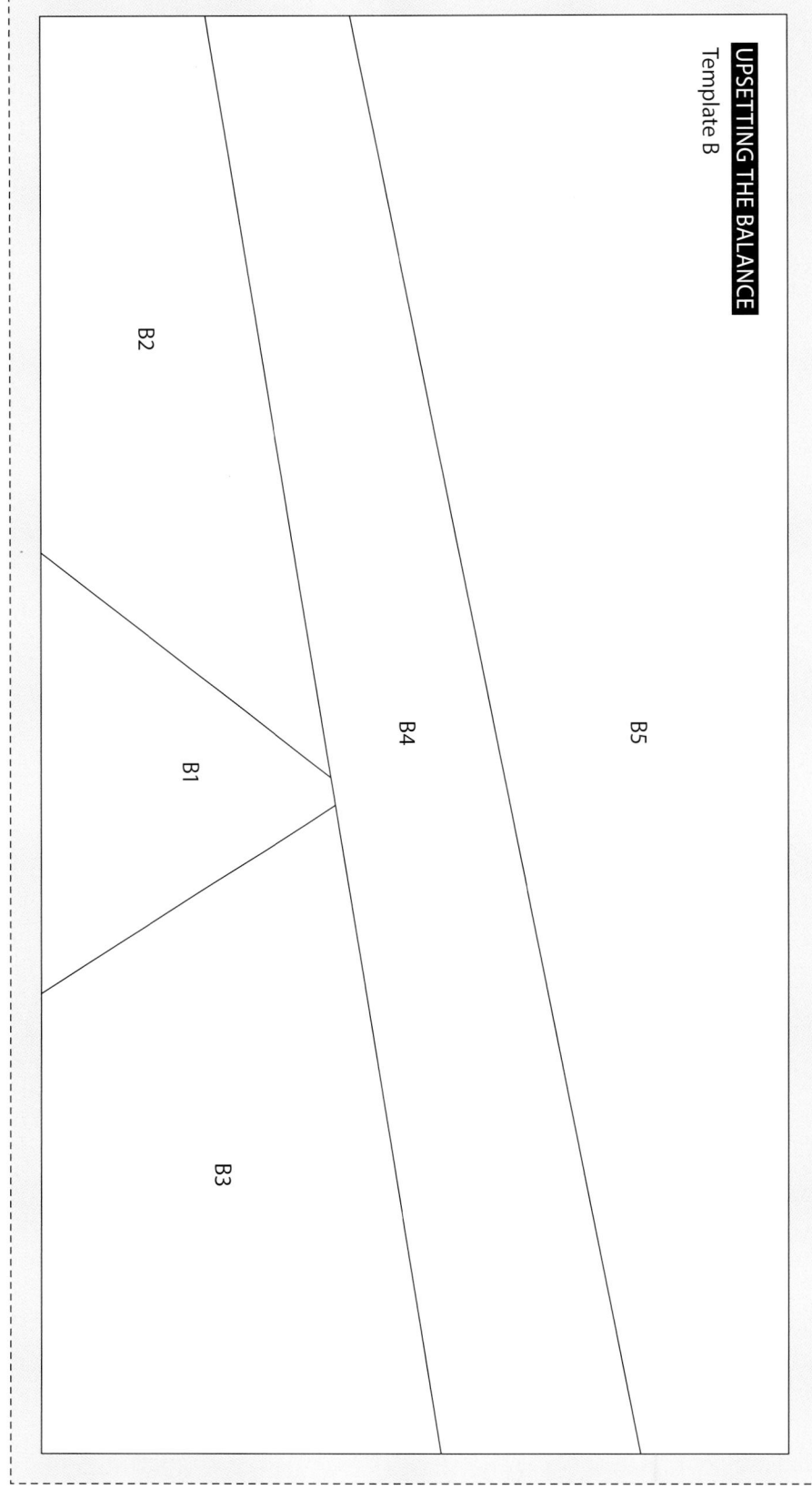

B2

B5

B4

B1

B3

Photocopy at 140%

- - - cut line

—— stitch line

░ seam allowance

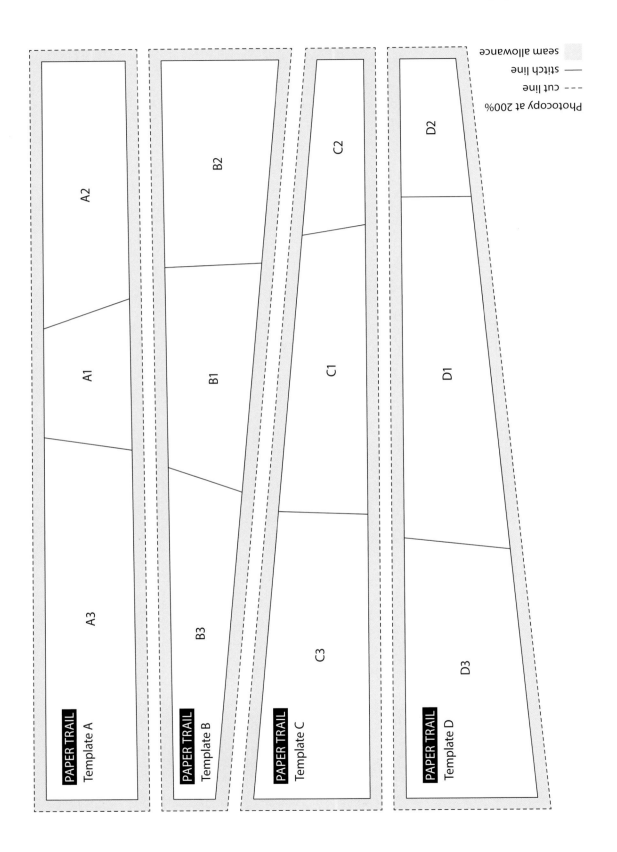

Photocopy at 200%
- - - cut line
——— stitch line
seam allowance

PAPER TRAIL
Template A

A2
A1
A3

PAPER TRAIL
Template B

B2
B1
B3

PAPER TRAIL
Template C

C2
C1
C3

PAPER TRAIL
Template D

D2
D1
D3

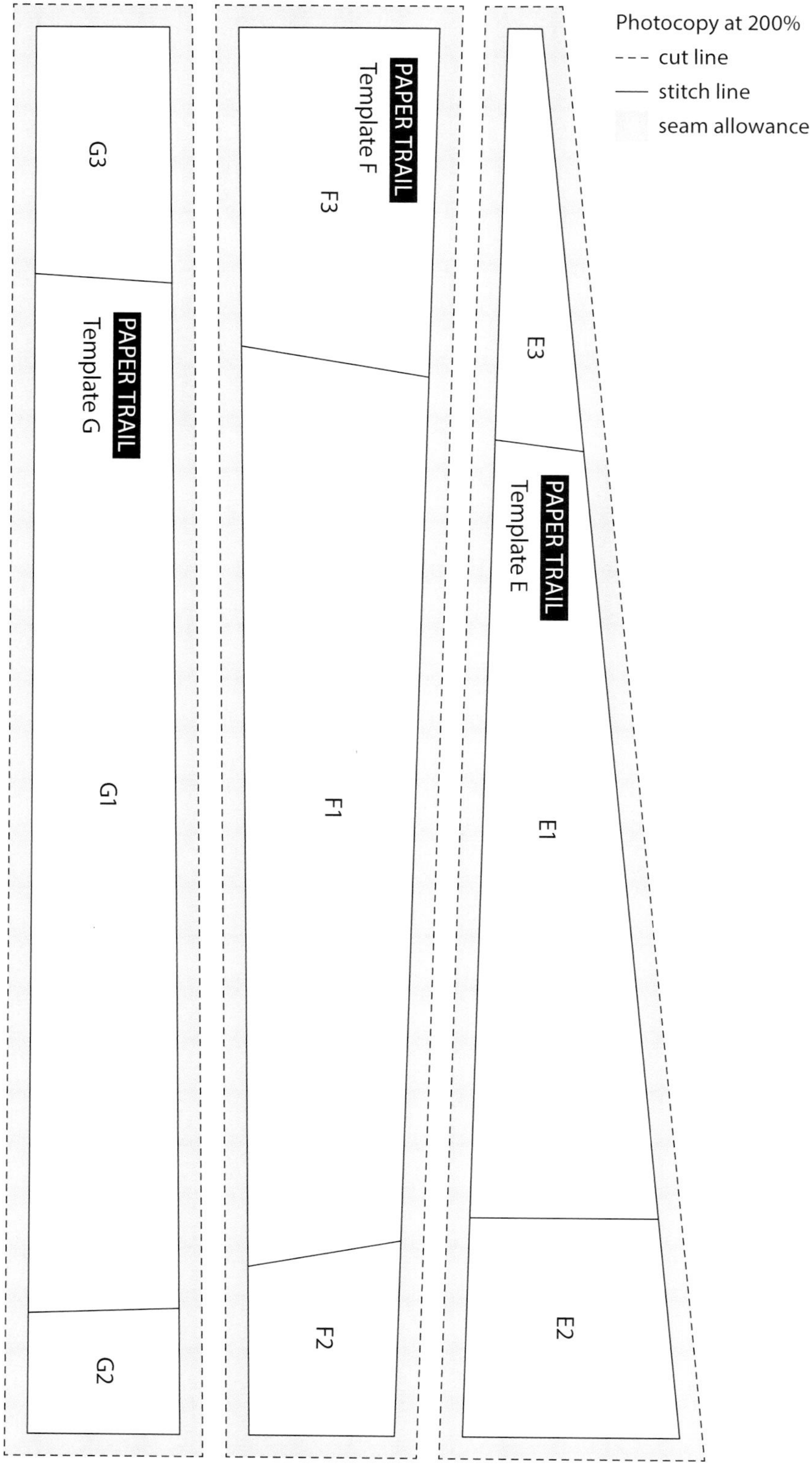

Photocopy at 200%

--- cut line
— stitch line
▢ seam allowance

G3

**PAPER TRAIL**
Template G

**PAPER TRAIL**
Template F

F3

G1

F1

**PAPER TRAIL**
Template E

E3

E1

G2

F2

E2

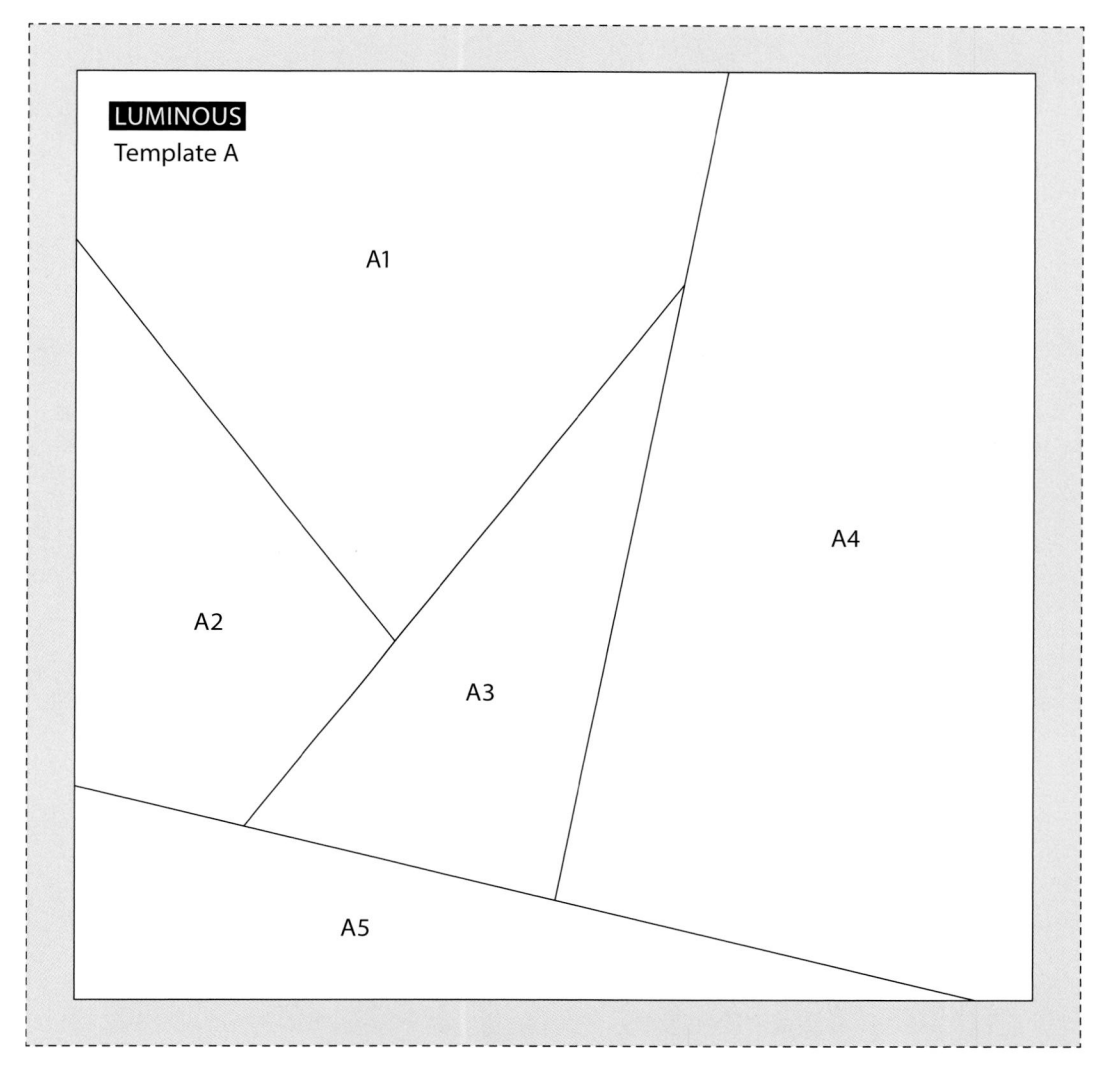

LUMINOUS
Template A

A1

A2

A3

A4

A5

Actual Size
- - - cut line
—— stitch line
seam allowance

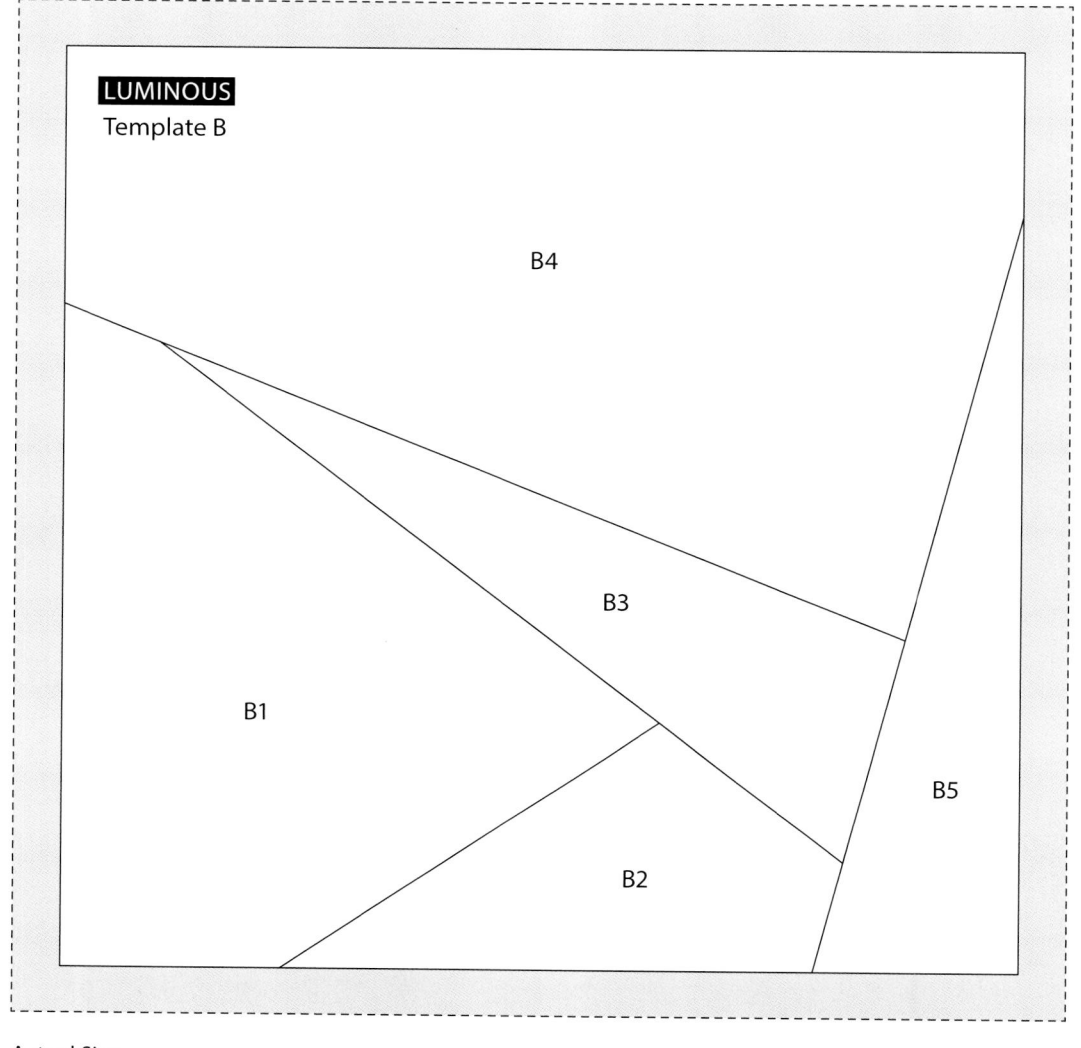

**LUMINOUS**
Template B

Actual Size
- - - cut line
—— stitch line
☐ seam allowance

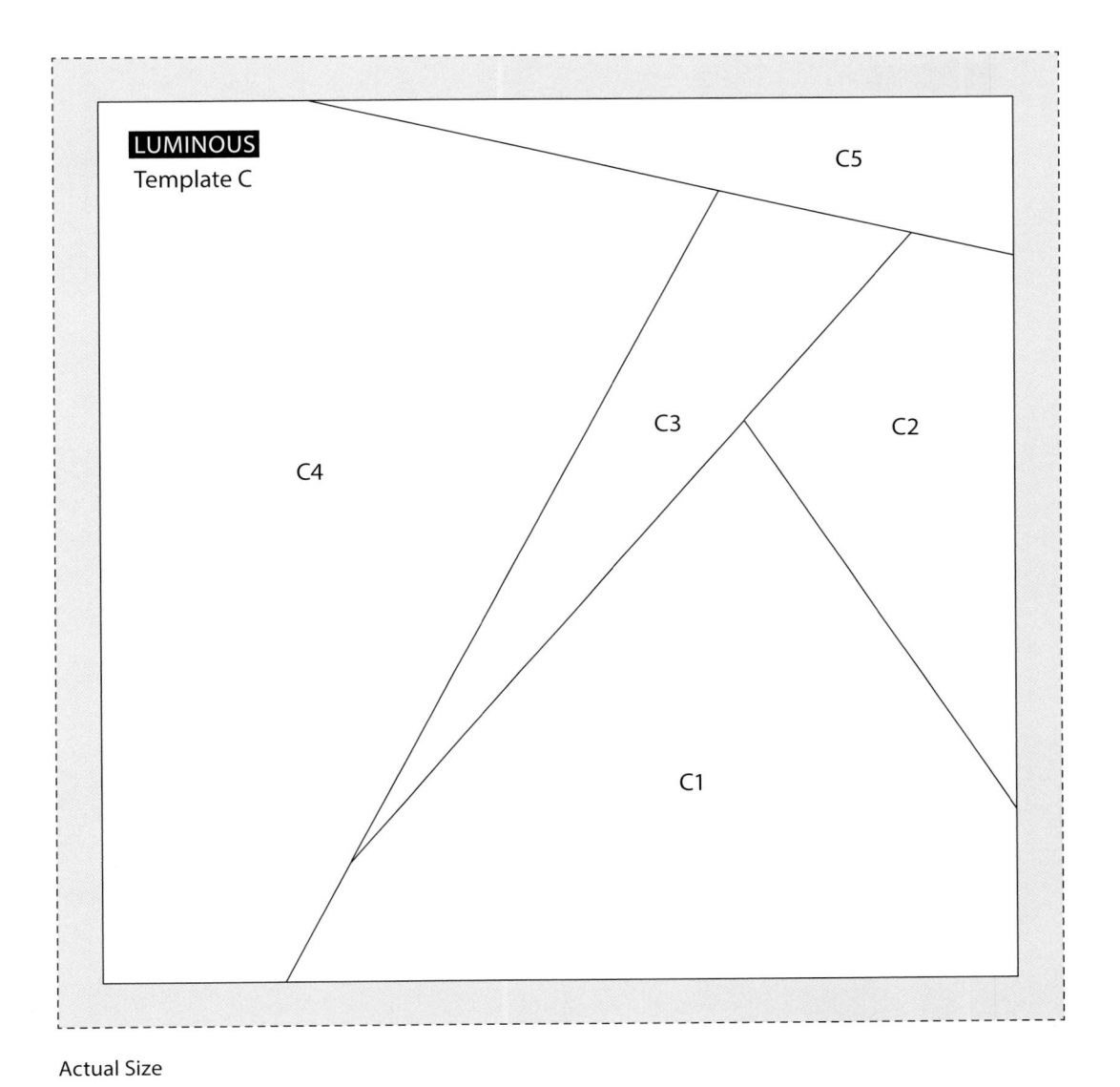

**LUMINOUS**
Template C

C5

C3

C2

C4

C1

Actual Size

- - - cut line

—— stitch line

seam allowance

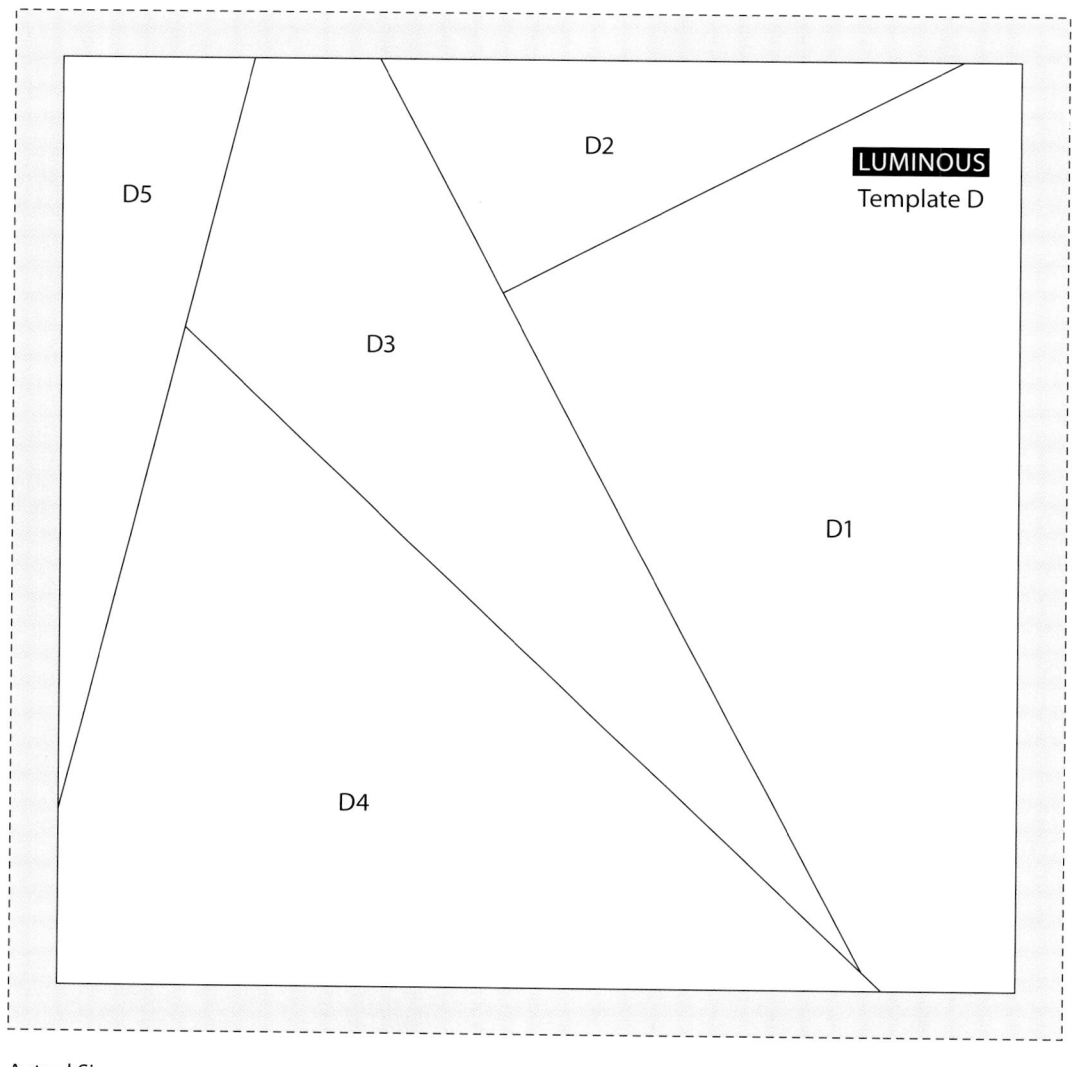

LUMINOUS
Template D

D5
D2
D3
D1
D4

Actual Size

- - - cut line
—— stitch line
    seam allowance

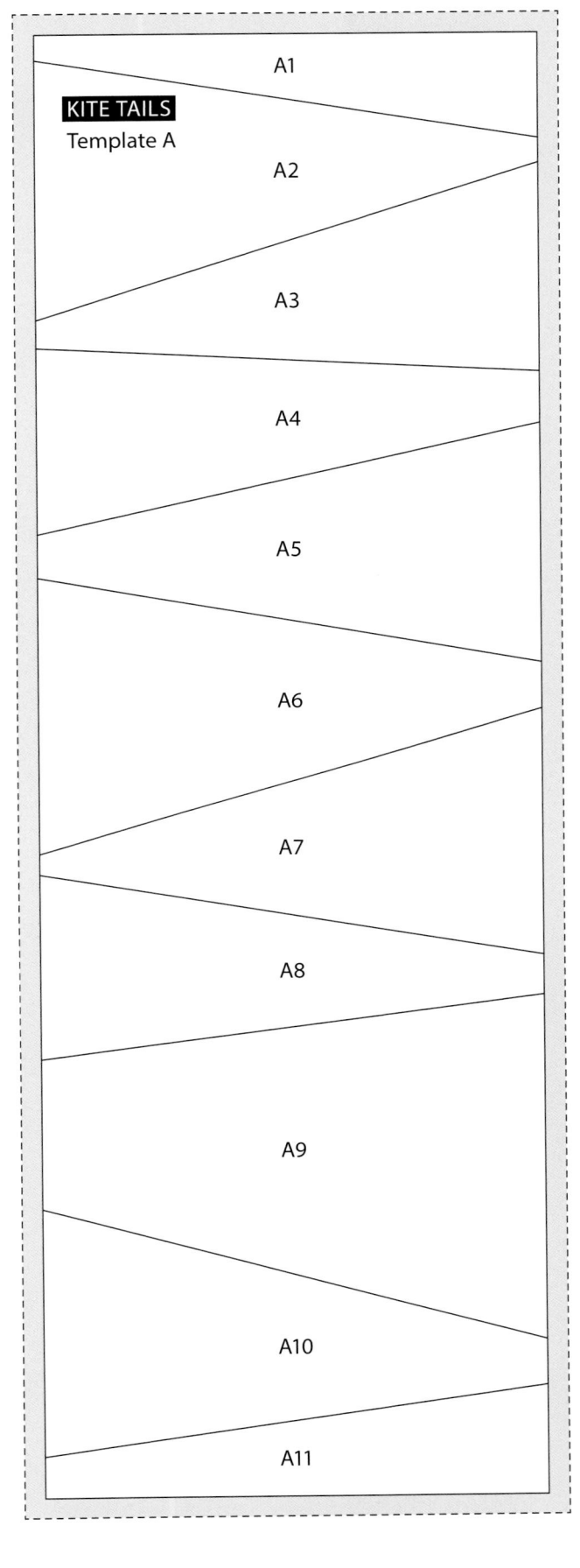

KITE TAILS
Template A

A1

A2

A3

A4

A5

A6

A7

A8

A9

A10

A11

Photocopy at 200%
- - - cut line
—— stitch line
▓ seam allowance

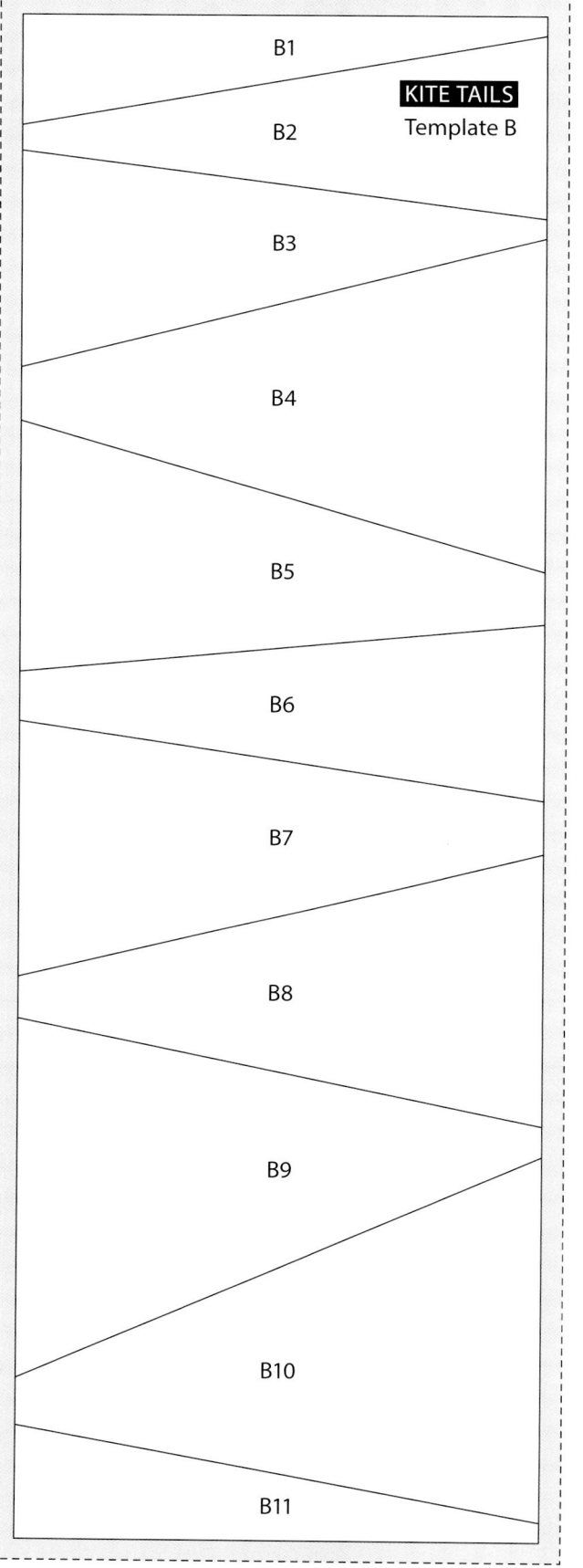

**KITE TAILS**
Template B

B1

B2

B3

B4

B5

B6

B7

B8

B9

B10

B11

Photocopy at 200%

--- cut line

— stitch line

  seam allowance

# Acknowledgments

Thank you to my family for understanding that my need to create will trump dusting every time. I love seeing my children's creativity flourish at our dining room table and I hope that they always find time to keep their creative side alive.

I would like to thank Susanne Woods for helping me to get my techniques and designs out into the world and for the free reign that she gives me to express my creative self. I appreciate the skill and expertise of all the members of the Lucky Spool staff who worked with me, especially Kristy Zacharias and Kari Vojtechovsky, who have shared their talents with me for a second time in the production of this book.

Thank you to Marianne Paley, who allowed me to use the Everett Mills, anchored in Lawrence's Downtown, for a photoshoot.

---

**AMY FRIEND** is an art historian and former museum collections curator who grew up sewing with her mother and grandmother, but didn't discover quilting until adulthood. With her growing family she left her full-time job to stay home and nurture her children, but soon realized she needed a creative outlet. In 2006 she began sewing again and blogging, and quickly became involved in the modern quilting movement.

She now expresses her creative side through sewing and pattern design. Amy enjoys the process of focusing on the thoughtful aspects of quilting—selecting proper fabrics, considering design placement and discovering the precise way to showcase her artistic vision. You can follow her on her website, duringquiettime.com.